D1601504

HOW TO STAY AHEAD
IN THE MONEY GAME

Also by James Jorgensen

The Graying of America
Your Retirement Income
How to Make IRAs Work for You

HOW TO STAY AHEAD IN THE MONEY GAME

James Jorgensen

STEIN AND DAY/*Publishers*/New York

First published in 1984
Copyright © 1984 by James Jorgensen
All rights reserved, Stein and Day, Incorporated
Designed by Louis A. Ditizio
Printed in the United States of America
STEIN AND DAY/*Publishers*
Scarborough House
Briarcliff Manor, N.Y. 10510

Library of Congress Cataloging in Publication Data

Jorgensen, James A.
    How to stay ahead in the money game.

    1. Finance, Personal—Handbooks, manuals, etc.
2. Investments—Handbooks, manuals, etc.   I. Title.
HG179.J63   1984   332.024   83-42974
ISBN 0-8128-2936-0

To my wife, Patricia

Acknowledgments

Books are rarely written alone.

I would like to thank all those from inside the banking, thrift, brokerage and mutual fund industries for their help, insight and ideas. I would especially like to thank Marie Stephens, who has been an important part of every book I have written, for reading and editing my manuscripts and for trying, desperately at times, to keep the subject within the grasp of every reader. And my wife, Pat. Without her support, this book could not have been written.

And last of all, this is dedicated to everyone who has helped me grow financially, to better understand not only money and how to accumulate it, but how thousands of you feel about it. Why it's important not to burn your bridges behind you, and, in today's confusing financial picture, how you should be able to adapt your strategy to changing situations.

Contents

Author's Note

The purpose of this book is to illustrate how our financial world is changing, how you can recognize the changes taking place, and where financial deregulation is taking us in a world of rapidly changing investing and saving opportunities.

We will cover a wide range of subjects—investments and where to save—and it will be impossible to cover each subject in detail. I'll try to give you a basic overview, but you should do your own study before you save or invest any money. No one can predict the future and there is no assurance or guarantee that you will have successful investments or secure savings if you follow any of the methods, strategies, or recommendations in this book. None of the material in this book should be construed as a personal investment recommendation, nor should you rely solely on what you read here. My purpose is to provide you with information you can use in planning your financial future in a world where the old rules have either changed or disappeared entirely. This is not a detailed guidebook.

If you have questions about your own personal investment or saving plan, you should consult with your accountant, attorney, retirement plan trustee, or other financial adviser.

Introduction

Here's something that'll get your blood boiling. Because banks and brokers are changing the rules, you could have thrown away 15 to 20% of your income last year through careless handling of your savings and taxes. Tax and investment laws are changing. Loopholes are slamming shut. Knowing where to save and how to profit from these uncertain times is crucial to your financial survival.

I want to show you how to do it.

Financial deregulation has been unleashed, and it's radically changing the way we have to think about money. Right now we're all lost in a maze of advertising. Every time you pick up the paper or turn on the television you find some guy crashing through the financial underbrush offering you pure gold. Or you get hit with gimmicks like a sweepstakes that will send you and your fancy new savings account floating away to a sandy beach in Hawaii. You feel like an idiot if you don't snap at these lures.

The problem is there's a lot of hoopla and not much good advice. With this book you can get your hands on the facts, stay clear of the ripoffs, and boost your savings by a whopping 25% a year . . . or more. You can earn back the price of this book every day and, most important of all, you'll be taking a substantial strain off the old fear bone that keeps you awake at night. In the lingo of finance, I want to give you the inside edge.

Financial supermarkets, zero bonds, mutual funds, banks, and thrifts drum into our heads: "Don't trust your company, don't trust your friends. You can't trust your government. Look out for yourself." They're right. Financially you need to look out for Number One. Nobody else is going to.

To do that, as you'll learn in this book, you've got to put your money where *you* can get it but *Uncle Sam* can't. Tough luck, Internal Revenue Service.

For years I wasted valuable time worrying about money—about all those new gimmicks I was missing, about diving into the market, about climbing out. Then it dawned on me. Basically, money worries come from uncertainty. Money is worrying stuff, no question about it, but I figured if I could throw out the uncertainty and lock onto the major principles of saving and investing money in today's confusing, fast-changing money market, I could build my nest egg in a handsome way, avoid some taxes, and get a good night's sleep.

The money market is changing fast. And you need to think seriously about using this change to your advantage. It's a worrisome prospect indeed: how to save, how to avoid (or at least minimize) taxes, how to shed old habits if you're going to survive in the decade of the eighties. Change is difficult. It rips away many of the ideas we've had since we first learned the importance of money.

Money *is* important. After sex, money is the most talked about, thought about, and dreamed about preoccupation in our lives. We need money for the good things—our homes, our cars, our vacations—not to mention the kid's orthodontist and the IRS on April 15. Until recently most of us squirreled away our money in saving accounts, where it earned minimal, government-controlled interest.

If you want to stay out of the financial quicksand, you'll need to keep one eye out for safety, of course, in a financial system that's undergoing swift change. But if you shop carefully when you save your money you can find ways to boost your savings 15 to 20% a year with a minimum of downside risk.

What I'm giving you in this book is a road map through the mine fields of financial deregulation and a way to make surprisingly high returns with almost the same safety as an FSLIC-insured account, to delay or save outright taxes you would otherwise pay on your earnings.

And I want to give you a real chance to help other members of your family boost their assets and make their money work as hard as they do.

Keep this book handy. Refer to it often. Mark it up. Like any good road map, it's meant to be used over and over.

The average saver's and investor's plight reflects today's stock market. Too many amateur crapshooters are playing the game. They not only don't understand how the game is played, they don't understand how the rules are changing. Brokers and mutual funds are moving into banking. The distinction between brokers, banks, and savings and loans blurs as we watch. Shearson, the big stockbroker, has been snapped up by American Express, the firm best known for its travel and entertainment credit card. Dean Witter, another large broker, has been acquired by Sears, which, with its in-store financial supermarket, is gunning for Middle America's pocketbook.

Big banks buy discount brokers, and move into the insurance business. Mutual funds, hoping to get on edge on banks, start their own national banks. Securities firms, insurance companies, even nonfinancial conglomerates, such as J. C. Penney and Kroger supermarkets, are making successful forays onto bank turf. Savings and loans elbow their way into stocks and bonds; car, home, and life insurance; credit cards, and checking accounts—even loans to help you buy a new or used car or boat.

This scramble for your dollars revolves around three laws. The fifty-year-old Glass-Steagall Act prevents banks from underwriting securities. The Bank Holding Company Act—pushing thirty —limits companies that own banks to activities judged by the Fed to be "closely related" to banking. And the almost sixty-year-old McFadden Act bars banks from jumping state lines.

The Treasury Department, in response to the mushrooming financial supermarkets and the strides of nonbank competitors, is moving aggressively to free banks from the restrictions of these laws so they can offer a full array of financial services. For starters, the Federal Reserve Board wants Congress to let banks set up mutual funds, underwrite government revenue bonds, underwrite and sell insurance, and offer real-estate investments, development, and brokerage. Soon you won't be able to tell the players without a scorecard.

For now, an army of lawyers are ferreting out ways around many of the existing restrictions. For example, the FDIC now contends that restrictions on banks' securities activities don't apply to the thousands of state-chartered commercial banks that aren't members of the Federal Reserve System.

In this decade you'll see about fifty major financial institutions, of which two dozen will be gigantic financial supermarkets, as opposed to the six thousand to eight thousand that we have now. You'll see five thousand, maybe more, thrifts simply disappear as the cost of carrying their expensive money palaces outraces the number of people who are willing to come in the front door. Giant banks and insurance companies will gobble up other businesses—

much as Bank of America absorbed the largest discount securities broker, Charles Schwab, and Prudential Insurance grabbed Bache Securities. The race for customers will spawn a new generation of fancy savings and investing plans . . . and marvelous opportunities to grab new ways to double or triple your money with safety.

Don't be surprised if you hear a friend bragging about thumbing his nose at the IRS with FSLIC-protected tax-free bonds wrapped in unit investment trusts paying the equivalent of 15 to 20%. Or maybe you'll hear of a company where employees fill their fringe-benefit plates from a Cafeteria Plan and then pay their bills with tax-free dollars that never show up on a W-2 form. Or your sister, who's considered an investment whiz, tells you that you can put as much as $15,000 into an individual SEP/IRA this year and then open another regular IRA and put the legal limit of $2,000 in *that* one. She may tell you that individual SEP/IRA limits will soon go higher.

You've got to keep up in the rapidly changing money game.

In the second half of this book you'll find something you rarely see in a money book: *practical advice on how to plan your own financial strategy.* But if you're going to have any chance of building a strong financial future, you've got to diversify your assets, widen your horizons, and watch over your money like a hawk.

I'll lay out for you a general financial strategy depending on your life situation, your age—and your personality. I'll show you where you can save taxes and maximize your tax-deferred income, where you should save or invest depending on your comfort zone. I'll try to give you an overall strategy, not specific investments. After all, neither I nor any other financial writer knows your personal situation, your family responsibilities, and, as we'll see, your inner feelings about money.

If you're between thirty and forty-five, you'll want to read chapter 7, "The Building Years: Make Megabucks, Spend Megabucks." If you're between forty-five and sixty you'll want to read chapter 8, "The Middle Years: Building a Solid Base." And if you're sixty-five or in retirement (or are worried about aging parents in this category) it's important to read chapter 9, "The Retirement Years: Don't Touch My Capital." It might even be a good idea to read all three, not just for your own sake but for other members of your family as well.

Part Two was obviously the most difficult part of the book for me to write. Most money books are heavy on what the writer wants you to know, light on what *you* need to do. That's because financial writers know our attitudes on saving and investing money vary widely. Often we are influenced by the turbulent economic times that shaped our particular generation. As a result, the way we handle money, and the way we save it to plan our financial future, often depends on how much of it we had while we were growing up.

So, how do you feel about money? This feeling, not how much you make or save, is going to influence you most when you plan your financial strategy to stay ahead in the money game. That's why we'll look at three different generations that make up America: the free-spending younger generation, the solid middle years after the children are grown, and the retired generation. Each of them faces the same economic and financial conditions although their feelings about money suggest they inhabit different worlds. And in many ways they do.

And another thing. Within each generation there are conservatives, risk-takers, and middle-of-the-road types. We'll look at them all.

Each generation came of age in a different economic era. Most Americans in the 1930s knew hard times but were never either destitute or rich. Prosperity climbed in the 1950s. In the early 1970s, comfort and plenty were assumed. Today's generation demands convenience. These are the people who will use the one-stop financial shopping centers of the future as a matter of course. They have more real purchasing power than their parents had at the same age, more income and credit to manage, and vastly higher material expectations.

Those in the solid middle years, with a decade or so to reach retirement, begin to feel anxious about their financial future. Their parents drilled into them during the Depression that both income and assets are precious. They must be protected; they could disappear quickly. These Americans' peak earning years began in an era of runaway inflation that saw the old work-save values dissolve like salt in the sea. Now, having acquired a home and a comfortable storehouse of money, they worry that inflation may reignite and blight their retirement years by eroding away much of what they have saved.

The retired older generation remains fearful of running out of money before they run out of breath. They have no new money in sight; they are afraid to touch their capital and they are, for good reason, interested in the safety of their assets. Their priorities often revolve around the three basic facts of life most of us take for granted: food on the table, a roof overhead, paid doctor bills. Many retired Americans, regardless of their financial wealth, still refuse to carry credit cards or incur any form of debt.

The decade of the eighties is forcing each generation to rethink its conception of money. With deregulation, the distinction between banks, thrifts, and insurance companies will soon be irrelevant. The country's most powerful financial institutions have declared war among themselves for a bigger share of the $3 trillion of saving and investing assets held by the public. Money is just another product to be merchandised, like detergent or white bread. Supermarkets, department stores, discount brokers hooked up by toll-free numbers—all lust after our cash with a blizzard of ads that leave us lost in a maze of conflicting claims.

For all their differences in outlook and needs, what the three generations are looking for, in a seemingly derailed financial world, is someone they can trust. In spite of the unprecedented number of financial products they have to choose from, most people are simply looking for savings and investments that will help them hold onto what they already have.

There's no point in getting overcomplicated about how saving and investing plans work, so I've given you the useful fundamentals. My advice comes from my days on Wall Street, where I learned how thin the financial markets really are in relation to their size and how unprotected they are from psychological shocks. I know that when panic hits, stocks that seemed rock solid one week can almost vanish the next.

My ideas and advice grew out of my work in pension and financial planning as well as from my research into the questions asked in the letters I've received from my previous money books. A good part of the understanding I have about money, however, comes from you, the American people. That's why my ideas and financial strategies, to a large extent, are based on the questions and ideas I've received on hundreds of radio and television programs around the country, the discussions and interviews I've had about money with people from all walks of life, and the hundreds of calls I've received on my CBS radio program, "The Financial Magazine." Another valuable source of insight into the world of money has come from the experts I've had on my program. Each with a special area of expertise, they've shed light on a variety of ways to save and invest money.

One thing I've learned about money is that you need to look behind the facts and figures. You need to find out what saving, investing, or paying of the mortgage can mean emotionally, not simply what they mean in dollars and cents. You must temper cold reason with the warmth of life experience.

Part of what I'll recommend also stems from my understanding of the basics—which are often more important than specifics on what and where to invest.

Before you begin, here are some principles about saving and investing to keep in mind as you read the book.

● Don't accept come-ons at face value. Check to see if you really have any long-term benefits after you invest. Then find out if you can defer taxes *before* you invest.

The chapter on IRAs is a good example of the powerful effect taxes can have at the start of any saving or investment period. If you and I both save the same amount of money at the same rate of return, and the only difference is that you don't pay any taxes and I do, on average it can take me *six years* in a 33% tax bracket to equal what you've earned in the *first year*. In a 50% tax bracket, almost *fifteen years*! Of course, my money will ultimately be returned tax-free and you'll eventually face the tax man, but if your objective is to build up a nest egg for the future, worry about paying the taxes after you have a pile of cash, not before.

● Don't let any financial institution con you into thinking it's doing you a favor by accepting your money. Consumer savings are one of the hottest commodities in the financial world. That's why it's important not to ignore the fine print and to find out what sales costs or commissions you'll pay. This is money off the top, money that will never have a chance to work for you. And above all, don't let yourself get handcuffed to an investment where heavy sales costs keep you from selling once the investment has gone sour. Of course, there are many good reasons why you might want to pay a sales commission, but consider the cost carefully before you invest.

Mutual funds are a good example. In chapter 4, you will learn that the average sales charge of 8% can reduce your average annual return for the first two years to only 1% a year! Hardly a way to stay ahead in the money game.

• Investigate your employer's fringe benefit package carefully. Look for ways to save with his help. The wave of the future will be in salary-reduction plans that will let you use, for necessary expenses and savings, money that doesn't show up on your W-2 form. Saving taxes in this way is like boosting your salary. The money you save could be a major factor in determining the size of your nest egg in future years.

• Pick an investment approach that's comfortable. No one stock has to be bought, no one investment has to be made. If you don't fully understand where you're being asked to risk your hard-earned cash, if you don't feel your broker or financial advisor has tilted the odds in your favor, back off. There is always another stock and always another day.

Everything I am advising you to do I have done myself or investigated for you. You will benefit most from this book if you already have some savings or assets, or if you can save part of what you earn, and you already own some property (like equity in your home). But you can benefit even if you have limited assets and they're locked up in a savings account.

You can start your personal and financial planning with as little as $50 or $100 a month. And you can save taxes and multiply your money on the same basis as the big investors.

Using my advice, you can knowingly pick your way through the financial underbrush and create a haven of stability and emotional security. The good news for us all is that we now enjoy a respite from inflation and, as savers, we enjoy high interest rates and unprecedented opportunities to save without government regulations.

What you invest in should make you happy. You should sleep at night without nightmares. For that reason, my suggestions and advice will try to gauge the risk for each investment along with the reward so you can tailor your financial plan, at least roughly, to your particular stage in life.

How to Stay Ahead in the Money Game is a book to keep handy. Use it regularly. It contains information you'll continue to need as new opportunities surface. Throughout the book you will find specific examples and tables to show what can happen to your money, how taxes can eat away a big chunk of what you believed you'd have when you retire. This is a no-nonsense self-help book on saving money and cutting taxes that I hope will keep you from wasting valuable time worrying about money.

So read on—while I do my best to sweep away the clouds that obscure your financial future.

PART ONE

1

CHANGES IN THE WAY WE SAVE: FROM BANKS TO SUPERMARKETS

Shortly after the Civil War the ruddy-cheeked son of a local newspaper editor and Confederate veteran became known around Lynchburg, Virginia, as "Pluck." The undersized youngster earned his nickname because, with eyes blackened and nose bloody, he had a way of fighting on against fearful odds.

Like his father, he became a small-town editor, fought for local issues in his paper, was elected to the state senate, and, in 1902, Virginia sent him to Congress. As a new member of the House, he was assigned to the Banking and Currency Committee. He knew nothing about finance, but "Pluck" was bent on learning. Ten years later, overcoming the odds he had fought all his life, he emerged the committee's chairman. He became a sponsor of the Federal Reserve Act, pushing it through the House in 1913.

When the Coolidge bull market collapsed, however, he became convinced that the Federal Reserve had been perverted from its original purpose of assisting legitimate business enterprise to manipulating the wildest stock speculation in history. Now a seventy-five-year-old senator, Carter "Pluck" Glass fought against even greater odds to repair the Federal Reserve. For two years he worked to perfect his reform bill as a companion piece to the Federal Reserve Act which he had pushed through the House of Representatives twenty years earlier. As he worked, "Pluck" could feel cold financial winds blowing in from Virginia—the flight of deposits from shaky banks, the scorn of the people for bankers and stockbrokers, the wholesale bank failures.

Senator Glass knew Roosevelt's New Deal would save its heaviest guns for regulating finance, to save a financial system that was near death. Even so, as his own bill to reform banking finally hit the Senate floor, cries of astonishment and alarm filled the chamber. The administration may have had some heavy guns, but the opposition had plenty of gunpowder, too. Private bankers warned that the Glass bill would rivet banks to a monstrous system of guaranteeing bank deposits. Whenever this had been tried, they said, it had been a disastrous failure. Senator Huey Long exulted, "The bill has no more chance to become law this session than I have to become Pope of Rome—and I'm a Baptist. It's dead as a hammer."

Undaunted, Carter Glass, one-time printer's devil and relentless reform campaigner, beat back a prolonged filibuster, kept his tongue and temper against fearful abuse, and, in the process, in February 1933, overcame the Senate's colossal inertia, and smiling benignly, saw the passage of his bill to reform the national banking system and tighten up loose screws in the Federal Reserve machine.

The bill's other author, Alabama's Henry Steagall, small-town lawyer and chairman of the House Banking and Currency Committee, spoke for those who wanted to save the "little" banks. Together these two men put their names on what has become known as the Glass-Steagall Banking Act of 1933, which gave President Roosevelt the most sweeping power over the U.S. pocketbook ever granted a president in peacetime.

"This bill has more lives than a cat," said a grinning president to Carter Glass, as he scrawled his name on the Glass-Steagall Banking Reform Act. "It has been declared dead almost fourteen times in the last few months and finally came through." In 1933, America was on its way back from the depths of the Great Depression. Banks would now be made safe. A new deal for money would spur the economy.

America was definitely on the move again. The most controversial part of the 1933 law was the bank-deposit-guarantee scheme, which most big city bankers said would never work. It was this "evil-smelling" trick of forcing big banks to pay a levy to guarantee the deposits of little banks that so outraged Manhattan bankers. But Glass's bill was written in such a way that it forced most banks into the Federal Reserve, creating one national system. He knew that once deposit-guarantee insurance came into effect, the public would withdraw their money from uninsured banks. And they did. Very few banks could do business outside the government's magic circle of deposit insurance.

Initially, deposits were to be guaranteed to a maximum of $2,500. After July 1934, deposits would be 100% guaranteed up to $10,000, 75% from $10,000-$50,000, and 50% above $50,000. The government was to launch this revolutionary enterprise by means of a new insurance company called the Federal Deposit Insurance Corporation (FDIC), which was to be financed by $150 million from the U.S. Treasury, with additional funds provided by the Federal Reserve Board Bank and by the individual banks. As it turned out, the banks themselves were the real guarantors. After initially putting .25% of their deposits into the insurance fund, they were required, whenever the fund sank below the required minimum level, to contribute another .25% of their deposits again and again, as long as they remained solvent.

Bankers ran in wild-eyed alarm. Deposits they had spent a lifetime to build up and protect with their good name could now be confiscated by the government and used to pay for the mistakes and dishonesty of every small-town banker. The American Bankers Association held the Act to be "unsound, unscientific, unjust, and dangerous."

In his book, *Money: Whence It Came, Where It Went,* John Kenneth Galbraith writes, "The dangers of the proposal [federal deposit insurance] were evident to all. The best banks would now have to accept responsibility for the recklessness of the worst. The worst, knowing that someone else would have to pay, would have a license for reckless behavior that the supervision authorized by the legislation could not hope to restrain . . . perhaps it [the FDIC] would mean a return to the wildest days of wildcat banking."

Instead, the new government insurance put the brakes to the panicky flight of desposits from banks, nine thousand of which had failed since 1929. In fact, the same day President Roosevelt asked Congress to legalize beer, healthy banks began reopening, and a financial system that was near death has scarcely had a sick day since.

The Glass-Steagall Act had one major provision: Banks were to get rid of their stock-selling business and get out of the investment business. With the 1929 stock market collapse fresh in their minds, millions of Americans wanted the banks barred from the stock market, wanted to keep them from using their millions to jeopardize the rebuilding of the financial community.

Banks had been participating in nearly two-thirds of all the new stock and bond issues, and the criticism was primarily aimed at such money-center giants as National City Bank of New York (the forerunner of Citibank) and Chase National (today's Chase Manhattan Bank). They were accused of lending money on a cut-rate basis to their own investment affiliates. Worse yet, many banks were known to have stuffed their trust departments with securities written by their own investment affiliates. It was even charged that the bank's own securities departments were trying to prop up the sagging stock prices of parent banks.

So great was the public outcry that several months before the Glass-Steagall Act became law, the major banks began to spin off their investment subsidiaries, and, when Senator Glass's bill was signed into law, J. P. Morgan and Company—the most august of all Wall Street names—decided to become a commercial bank. Now faced with a decision between banking and the securities business, most of the big financial institutions chose to stay where the money was—in the bank. Ironically, Wall Street, which has become the villain as the 1929 Crash has grown to mythical proportions in the American mind, got off relatively lightly at first. The Securities Act of 1933, the first federal securities legislation, merely required companies that sold securities to the public to make full disclosure of all material relevant to the offering. The regulatory crunch did not hit Wall Street until early in 1934 when Congress completed its investigation into the causes of the Crash. Then, as the public began to grasp the depth of the stock scandal, an irrational distrust of people who appeared to manipulate the securities market sprang up in this country. An outraged Congress enacted the Securities Exchange Act of 1934. Unlike its predecessor, this law had real teeth. It put the exchanges under federal oversight, limited margin buying, and created the Securities and Exchange Commission (SEC) to police Wall Street and the overall investment market.

To head the SEC, President Roosevelt picked Joseph P. Kennedy, Jr., father of the late president John F. Kennedy. The Boston Irishman had made millions by speculating in the stock market during the 1920s and presumably knew all the tricks of the trade he was being asked to police. The SEC's main function was to give investors confidence that the financial markets would never again be manipulated as they were before the Crash.

Now, fifty years later, banks again yearn to underwrite bonds. "Municipal revenue bonds are the wave of the future," said a Senate Banking Committee staffer, "and banks want to get in on it." States and cities believe they could cut their financing costs if the banks made a limited return to the securities business. Banks believe that a return to underwriting securities can only be a prelude to full competition with the likes of Dean Witter and Merrill Lynch.

So far, in this new free-for-all climate, technological change and deregulation of commissions have allowed anyone to set up his or her own fee schedule and to buy and sell securities at cut-rate prices. This has caused a new phenomenon to emerge on the financial scene—the discount broker. Because discount brokers only buy or sell securities and do not offer investment advice and underwrite stocks and bonds, these new players in the money game can under-cut the commissions of established, full-service brokers by as much as 70% by offering strictly cut-rate, no-frills service.

When discount stockbrokers were seen to be grabbing a growing share of the commissions investors pay to trade securities, the big banks began to eye this new money machine. Although according to the Glass-Steagall Act, banks and thrifts may not hold securities in their own name, offer new issues, make a market in any stock or bond, or offer research or advisory service, they can trade securities at bargain prices and hopefully attract the upscale customers back into their money store.

For banks and thrifts, hard hit by aggressive competition from brokers and mutual funds, this was what they had been waiting for. The nation's largest banks and thrifts began to offer discount brokerage services. By the spring of 1983, there were about a thousand depository institutions offering some form of discount brokerage service, and their number will grow among the nation's seventeen thousand banks and forty-five hundred savings and loans.

But banks and thrifts are not alone. New England Mutual Life Insurance Company allows its agents to offer discount brokerage services. The company expects its life insurance customers will choose to trade securities through New England Mutual Life because they know and trust its agents.

It's as if Senator Glass had taken his foot off the brakes and now the money gatherers appear headed for a major collision, tearing down the barriers that once protected the securities business from the banks and thrifts. The banks "were mad as hell," I was told by one banker, because Glass-Steagall had been keeping them out of the securities business while their competitors were free to snap up brokerage houses at will. For example, Prudential Insurance Company of America acquired Bache and Company, one of the nation's largest full-service brokerage firms. Sears acquired Dean Witter, and American Express bought up Shearson. Ultimately, the chances of keeping the banks and thrifts out of the full-service securities business are meager at best. The simple pecking order requires that they be included.

Bankers have another worry that winds back to a time just before the Great Depression, before the 1933 Banking Act, when the big banks first began to branch out into small-town America. Until that time, this country's banking system had grown up on single-unit banks. Because branch banks were almost unknown, neither the National Bank Act nor the Federal Reserve Act gave specific mention to branches. A few banks had them, but they were the exception. It was not until after World War I that branch banks began to dot the landscape, and by 1925 branch banking had become a hot issue.

Congress began to hear the cries of virtually every small-town banker and hoisted a red warning flag toward the rapidly spreading banking giants, putting the skids on nationwide banking. The McFadden Act was passed in 1927 to "further amend the National Banking Laws and the Federal Reserve Act, *and for other purposes.*" It prohibited interstate banking, and for almost sixty years it has barred banks from jumping state lines.

The Act was a victory for two small-town bankers, Representative Louis T. McFadden (R-Pa.) and Senator George W. Pepper (R-Pa.), who were concerned that big-city banks could invade their turf and steal their customers. Scenting the direction of the political wind in 1926, McFadden and Pepper played to the emotional issue of brick-and-mortar branch banking where big city banks invade local communities with fancy bank buildings and force smaller banks to give up a major share of their customers to the big-city competitors.

For decades, this bit of protectionist history was the glue that held the banking business together. By controlling competition and limiting the interest they could pay on their customers' deposits, bankers had a key to Fort Knox. Often managers, who were little more than caretakers of a protected money machine, could be found on the golf course.

Then came the sixties. Almost overnight banks caught fire, going after retail business they had let slip away and expanding overseas, away from federal regulations, and, in a radical break with their past, buying money instead of waiting for it to come through the door. They began to offer Negotiable Certificates of Deposit (CDs), enabling them to outbid everyone else for money. In banking jargon, a certificate of deposit is a financial instrument that evidences the placement of a sum of money with a bank for a specific time period at an agreed-upon rate of interest. Looking for big chunks of money, banks began to offer attractive rates for Jumbo CDs of $100,000 or more.

The rise of bank-issued CDs was a quiet revolution, but it changed the banking industry forever. Before the advent of buying deposits, bankers knew how much money was in the bank and how much the cost of the interest would be to keep it there. Their business plan was simple: lend out what they had at the best interest rate they could get. But when banks began to buy money, two new things began to happen: they could no longer predict the future cost of the money they had bought because CD rates rose and fell with the market rate demand, and there was no longer any limit on the amount of money they could buy or the number of loans they could make. "It was as if a dam broke," one banker said. Another called it "mindless lending." The more loans they made, the bigger their profits.

In 1960, banks held twice as much in demand deposits, "free money," as in time and saving deposits. By 1966, they held more locked-in time/saving deposits than free money. Today, the proportion is even better, more than three to two in favor of purchased money, with 50% of their deposits in the money-grabbing idea that started it all: certificates of deposit. The biggest problem banks have today is not what to do with our savings accounts, but where to find the mounting billions they need to continue to cover their enormous outstanding loans. Many of these are to Third World or underdeveloped countries that can clearly never repay their debts.

With the value of outstanding bank CDs soaring from $26 billion at the end of 1970 to more than $132 billion at the end of 1981, the old saying about banks bears repeating: If you owe them $5,000, they own you; if you owe them $500 million, you own them.

The seventies brought something Pluck Glass could never have foreseen: swift technological change. With computers and electronic banking, the restrictive laws of the 1930s began to bite even harder, acting as a drag on the whole economy and putting financial institutions into a straitjacket to fit conditions that no longer existed. Once more the forces that had caused the previous stress, the public's right to a better deal, began to creep and gather. By the start of the eighties, the government-protected banking system no longer fit what the world had become. The stress and strains grew great, and we again began a reordering of our financial institutions to meet the new realities.

Today, as they bid for middle-market customers, the banks, big and small, are no longer fighting just among themselves for their share of the market; they are fighting a new and growing group of "nonbanks" and "near-banks," as well. These other financial institutions have made an end run on the McFadden Act in the belief that the law applies only to banks.

Credit unions, many savings and loans institutions (S&Ls), and even mutual funds, in effect, make loans, accept deposits, and allow checks to be drawn against them without geographical restrictions. The savings and loan industry is moving ahead on the grounds that the McFadden Act, written for banks, does not cover thrifts. If you live in California, New York, or Florida, you can see the brick and mortar of Nationwide Savings and Loan, a thrift that has jumped state lines and is about to expand again.

The most interesting breach of the McFadden Act occurred in 1982, when Fidelity Savings and Loan Association, a large Northern California thrift, was forced to close its doors by the Federal Home Loan Bank Board. Fidelity Savings was considered "large" by S&L standards, and it was determined that it would cost the Federal Savings and Loan Insurance Corporation (FSLIC) huge sums of money to keep the financial house from collapsing.

If only some major financial institution could be induced to step in and assume some of Fidelity Savings's huge debt, the FSLIC could save the depositors' money and cut its losses at the same time. Casting around for a white knight to save Fidelity, the FSLIC turned to New York's Citicorp, the second largest bank in the country. Citicorp had the deep pockets necessary to rescue Fidelity Savings and get the FSLIC off the hook at the same time.

The banking giant was irresistibly drawn by the FSLIC's offer: the chance at last to jump state lines, a clear erosion of the McFadden Act. Fidelity Savings is now called Citicorp Savings, and Citicorp has, in effect, leaped across state lines from New York to California as a first step into interstate banking.

Then in 1983, Bank of America, already the nation's largest bank, set out to acquire Seattle-First National, the largest bank in the Pacific Northwest. Seafirst had been stung by the failure of the Penn Square Bank of Oklahoma City, which dropped $400 million of bad loans on its books, and it was in danger of closing its doors. To forestall its insolvency, the FDIC wanted to arrange a merger that would pump some badly needed cash into the bank. Washington state, eager to keep its biggest bank from collapse, quickly passed a new law allowing an out-of-state bank takeover.

Congress has been reluctant to step in and change the federal laws banning interstate banking, except where states specifically authorize it, because the political influence of the small banks, which make up most of the 14,500 commercial banks, could be expected to generate considerable opposition to any change. "Congress prefers to let it happen, to let the market make the changes," believes economics professor Edward Kane of Ohio State University. "If no one protests too loudly, then Congress will add its stamp of approval." Kane also thinks that "the federal laws against interstate banking have looked silly for quite a while."*

There's an interesting historical footnote to Bank of America's current interest in Seafirst. A. P. Giannini, Bank of America's founder, was known for his ambition to branch out across the nation. He once attempted to buy Citibank's predecessor bank. He did buy a small New York bank called Bank of America and promptly changed the name of his California bank from the Bank of Italy to the Bank of America. Later, his continued focus on the New York market led to a well-known meeting with J. P. Morgan, during which they reached an agreement that "New York was for J.P., the West for A.P."

In offering to buy Seattle-First National, Bank of America agreed

---

*The Wall Street Journal, April 26, 1983.

to supply $150 million cash and buy the bank for $125 million cash and $125 million of a new type of Bank of America preferred stock. The most innovative feature, and one that could speed up even faster the arrival of full interstate banking, was the offer to exchange Seafirst common for Bank of America's preferred stock. The preferred's value can be reduced if Seafirst's losses on certain existing loans exceed $50 million. "It's a way," a Seafirst banker said, "of protecting [Bank of America] shareholders against a bottomless pit."

What it will also do is link the largest banking organizations in California and Washington state and spur the current trend toward interstate banking. Interstate banking is coming, not because the McFadden Act has been repealed, but because the importance of rescuing failing thrifts and banks overrides our concern about the menace of nationwide banking, and because state legislatures are tearing down the barriers against interstate banking. By 1983, at least nine states, from Alaska to New York, now allow out-of-state bank holding companies inside their borders. Some, such as Delaware, South Dakota, Virginia, and Nebraska, ban foreigners from competing with local banks. By 1984, at least one state in three will allow some kind of banking across state lines.

Not to be outdone by the banks, the Federal Home Loan Bank Board (the federal regulators of the savings and loans) wants to give thrifts the right to merge or open branches across state lines where state laws permit. Many states already allow interstate branching of state-chartered institutions, and if federally chartered institutions aren't allowed to do the same thing, they could be at a disadvantage in the mad rush to jump state lines. A staff report spelled out the board's actions in these concise words: "The board was reconsidering its past policy in the light of rapid changes taking place in the whole field of financial services and against the background of the financial crisis recently facing thrift institutions."

But the cost of protection comes high. The nation's banks and thrifts, sheltered under an umbrella of restrictive federal laws, now find themselves with too many similar types of institutions competing for the same piece of the pie. Pluck Glass, with the public's outcry to make banks safe ringing in his ears, had built the wall too high.

The glue that held the financial community together for over fifty years came unstuck at the beginning of the eighties. Ingenuity in finding ways around the laws enabled bankers to "grow by loopholes," paying interest on demand deposits and, as we've already seen, operating across state lines. Stretching loopholes to the limit, banks and near-banks, such as Sears and American Express, continued to fight ferociously to attract the consumer's dollar. By 1982, a head-on collision between giant banks and near-banks was taking shape. With institutions such as Citibank and Sears battling toe-to-toe for the consumer's pocketbook, something had to give, and that something was the nation's archaic regulatory wall that separated one type of financial institution from another.

Bankers had talked about deregulation for years, but the need at least to abolish interest-rate ceilings took on a new urgency when inflation-bedeviled depositors began yanking out their cash and putting it into the nonregulated money market funds. In four years, between 1977 and 1981, money fund assets climbed an astounding 17,200%, while bank savings deposits fell 24% and those of thrifts, 35%.

As a result, after years of congressional infighting, a sweeping overhaul of the nation's banking system emerged from the legislative mill: the Depository Institutions Deregulation and Monetary Control Act of 1980. In an all-out effort to bring the banking industry into the electronic age, Congress legislated a six-year phase-out of interest rate ceilings and turned the various members of the financial community into direct competitors for the first time since the Great Depression.

Decisions as to the timing and speed of change were left to a new deregulation committee composed of the Secretary of the Treasury, the chairman of the Federal Reserve, FDIC, Federal Home Loan Bank Board (for the S&Ls), and National Credit Union Administration, and the comptroller of the currency (non-voting). The committee must meet at least once a quarter, in open session, and complete the job of deregulating the banking business by 1986.

But once unleashed, even gradually, financial deregulation began to spread like wildfire, sweeping away interest rate ceilings, boosting federal deposit insurance from $40,000 to $100,000, allowing thrifts to offer checking accounts, and making it easier for nonbanks to buy or start up a money machine of their own.

The banking industry itself began to unravel as deregulation picked up speed, cutting across supposedly unbreachable protective walls and spreading to the securities, thrift, and insurance industries. The customer was king. Rates and fees plummeted and interest rates on savings soared. Banks and thrifts were forced to cut their costs. For the first time since Senator Glass gave them a protected money machine, they were pinching pennies to survive.

No one in the financial community doubts that the pace of deregulation will hasten in the years to come. Banking deregulation has spread beyond the controls it was designed to loosen. It opened doors to nonbanking companies, allowing them to establish regular banks and nonbanks.

The comptroller of the currency, picking up the mood of the administration, began to ease the rules on who could buy or start a bank. The big mutual funds, hurt by a lack of insurance on their money funds, were allowed to set up national banks. Industrial companies such as Gulf and Western and Parker Pen were allowed to set up their own banks. Anyone, it seemed, with sufficient capital, management, and a business plan could open a national bank. As a result, in the decade of the eighties, mom-and-pop banks are sprouting like weeds.

Until recently, recipients of national bank charters were protected from competition for several years. No neighboring start-up bank would be approved without first demonstrating "economic need" for a nearby bank. "Only a fool could lose money," a banker said, "but that's all changed." In fact, deregulation became so wild that banking turned into love seats, box springs, and banking. Richard McMahan, owner of the seventy-three-store McMahan furniture chain, wanted a bank in order to sell his beds and chairs on credit to his more than one hundred thousand installment loan customers. The U.S. comptroller's office, issuer of national bank charters, enthusiastically agreed. In what may be a model for specialized branch banking of the future, McMahan opened his first bank in 1983; he hopes to have at least fifteen in his stores in five years, while scattering automated teller machines among the chain's other in-state locations.

By 1982, with regular banks and thrifts still under tight government control on interest rates and saving plans, investors began to pour cash into money market mutual funds at the torrid rate of $300 million a day. With Wall Street in a deep slump, and gold and silver prices on the skids, the money market funds were the only game in town, offering an average yield of 14%. Concerned that banks and thrifts were falling off the pace as the nation's leading money gatherers, the new Depository Institutions Deregulation Committee, moving up its deregulation schedule, in December 1982 allowed banks and thrifts to introduce a new, insured, money market account that ripped the ceiling off low, government-set account yields. They began to offer interest rates three percentage points higher than money-market funds, and millions of dollars of slick advertising purchased deposits that cost them more than they could earn.

By October of 1983, federal financial regulators voted to reduce minimum-deposit requirements and lift the interest ceilings on term deposits with maturities of thirty-two days or longer. The Depository Institutions Deregulation Committee has now established the final wave of financial deregulation by offering the following schedule.

Beginning December 1, 1983, minimum deposits will be eliminated for all accounts used in tax-deferred individual retirement accounts (IRAs).

Beginning January 1, 1984, banks may increase to 5.5% the interest they pay on passbook savings accounts, the same rate currently offered by savings & loans.

Beginning January 1, 1985, the current minimum deposit of $2,500 will drop to $1,000 for all money market savings accounts and for deposits with maturities of seven to thirty-one days and no-rate-limit "Super-Now" accounts.

Beginning January 1, 1986, minimum deposit requirements will be eliminated entirely.

Banks and thrifts were ill-prepared for the new no-holds-barred competition. Among other things, they were saddled with enormous and expensive buildings, money palaces built at a time when concrete substance meant safety. These were once grand gatherers of cheap deposits. Now they became heavy cost burdens in a rapidly deregulated marketplace. Many branches, too, are haphazardly located; their drive-up windows and fancy lobbies remain half-empty. Bankers, preoccupied with creating new accounts and luring customers with big bonuses, soon discovered that paying high interest rates as well as high rents and wages meant disappearing profits. Clearly, the decade of the eighties will see a marked reduction in the number of brick-and-mortar bank and thrift branches. Many will melt into metal money-machines fastened on the side of a wall.

Small- to medium-sized regional firms, locked into the past, will have the toughest time since they have neither the economies of scale nor the capital market clout of the bigger banks, or the customer loyalty and location that help small community banks. Many will soon be closing up shop. But if banks and thrifts begin to devour each other, the public can hardly be expected to shed tears. The surviving stockholders, enriched for generations by one of the last officially sanctioned monopolies in America, can sell out at a price that would have made the founders faint dead away.

The banks and thrifts that survive will raise their fees, impose penalties, charge for their services, increase the fine print in their advertising—for services that used to be subsidized by low saving- and checking-account yields. "Speaking from the heart and not the wallet," a banker told me, "I tell my friends not to be swayed or impressed by all the advertising flurry and noise. In the long run, the banks offering the most now will either stick on the high charges or go broke."

But low-overhead, technologically advanced money centers are spelling trouble in an increasingly fee-oriented business. They will set the benchmark price for service, not the old brick-and-mortar firms. Money market mutual funds are a case in point. They offer a wide range of saving and investing plans—taxable, tax-free, and tax-deferred—and still make a tidy profit because they combine toll-free numbers, top-notch technology and low cost overhead. Brokers are another example. They already offer most of the customer services of banks and thrifts, yet they spread their costs over a wide range of products and pay their money gatherers a straight commission.

What's more, for the first time, the government will give all the money gatherers the freedom to fail. As one banker said, "For years the federal government told us how to operate. They gave us our instruments and priced them for us, then told us to go out and make a lot of executive decisions on how many pots and pans we were going to give away. Now we're being placed in a more free enterprise environment." What's more, banks and thrifts will have to catch up, compete for the savers' dollar with competitive interest rates and services, and move rapidly into the nonbanking financial services—insurance, stocks and bonds, money management accounts, real estate, commodity trading, even the opening of travel agencies.

To put the plight of the banks and thrifts into perspective: about 80% of their saving deposits come from 20% of their depositors—those in the upscale category—and maybe 75% of those depositors have been pirated away by the big brokers with their cash management accounts. This is why it's so important for banks and thrifts to become competitive, now that they are free of government control.

Banks and thrifts are going to have to catch up in a hurry. Investors and savers are becoming better educated, more sophisticated, and less inclined to let a cowboy on television advise them on money matters. It's also clear that the competition will go where the customers are. Sears, Penney's, Kroger supermarkets, and other retail stores, gunning for Middle America's pocketbook, have acquired brokers, thrifts, and insurance companies. The entry of Kroger, the nation's second largest food chain, into the money game is an example of how far the wheels have fallen off the banks' well-oiled savings machine.

The grocery list of the future could well include a dozen eggs, a quart of milk, an oil filter, and a homeowner's insurance policy. Food retailers across America are being urged to offer auto and home insurance as well as mutual funds along with the fresh vegetables and the Tide. "Car and home insurance are already regarded as commodities by customers, who perceive little difference among insurance companies—and they are right," says a supermarket consultant. "Quality, convenience, and price are what sell insurance policies these days." Many supermarket owners believe that the key to selling insurance and offering financial services is the salaried sales force within the store. The continuous presence of these agents bolsters consumer confidence because they know someone is always available to answer their questions. And bankers, eager to cut the exploding cost of paperwork, are rushing to put teller machines next to the frozen foods.

Kroger, for its part, has spurned the high rent of a banking palace and opened three-hundred-square-foot financial centers in their food stores to offer insurance, mutual funds, money market funds, check writing, and other financial services. To reduce money to its simplest form, a computer takes the shopper's financial history when he or she enters the store and presents a custom-tailored saving, investing, and insurance plan by the time the customer has finished shopping. What makes financial supermarkets like Kroger's and Sears's important is not that they are now permitted under the changing money game, but that they can offer all these services to the public for a start-up cost of $25,000-$50,000—less than 5% of what it costs to do business from the current banking palaces.

"What we're going to have," one thrift executive told me, "is a boom in the number of small, very low-cost branch offices. They'll be staffed by two or three people and tied into our computer; that is, before we junk the whole system and go for the electronic teller machines and do away with the branch offices altogether."

Today, however, what most banks and thrifts have as they face this challenge to once again woo the saver's dollar, are high-priced office buildings and the transaction business—an unprofitable bummer.

Like most people, I've become accustomed to high levels of personal service where I bank and a branch on every street corner. But heavy cost burdens of playing on a level playing field will mean the end of banking services as we know them today. Citibank calculates that to operate its bank it costs $100 a year for each customer it serves and a mere $20 for an automatic teller machine. In Philadelphia, a bank charges thirty cents to withdraw money from a human teller and only ten cents from a machine.

In the decade of the eighties, the fast-moving, volatile world of money will require that all of us become knowledgeable savers and investors. We'll have to learn not to put our money in one pocket and let taxes take it out of the other. Uncle Sam has a voracious appetite for money to keep the government afloat. Being a bully in the crowd around the money well, government often can compete more favorably for our money than the banks and thrifts it set adrift in a sea of competitive sharks. After all, it makes up the rules on how money works. And this gives us opportunities to invest in virtually risk-free government securities.

Consider this. One morning, out of the corner of my eye, I saw a television ad that captured the confusion of our age. A well-dressed, older man, wearing a three-piece suit and the purposeful look of a financial genius, paused on a sidewalk in the middle of a busy downtown financial center and said into the camera, "If you want safety and high yield for your hard-working money, open our insured Super Money-Market Account paying a high 9%. I used to think I had to risk my money in the market for this kind of return." Then, with the exaggerated mannerism of a 60-second commercial, he shook his head as if to say, "No way." Or maybe he shook his head because he doesn't understand the rules any more.

What the man with the expensive suit didn't say was that, with the same amount of savings, you could have earned 10% on your money through a broker or mutual fund. Better yet, your 10% would be tax-free if you invested in tax-free bonds. In a one-third tax bracket (where most of us find ourselves, particularly with a two-spousal income) that's like earning 15% interest—almost twice the rate paid by the smiling man on television.

But what about safety, you ask? The 9% money market account is insured by the FSLIC up to $100,000. The 10% tax-free bonds are also protected by the FSLIC, up to $100,000. In fact, the tax-free bonds could have been secured by the same thrift institution's certificates of deposit that brought you the expensive commercial offering 9% and the chance to give a big chunk of your interest income back to Uncle Sam. Earning 15% instead of 9%, with the same safety and liquidity—that's the right stuff!

The saving mess we're in can be laid at the government's doorstep. Undoing decades of tight saving controls all at once is creating massive confusion—and opportunities. In the long run, the saver will benefit as banks, thrifts, brokers, and mutual funds broaden their services and essentially become the same type of saving and investing institution. The good news is that financial deregulation will open up unprecedented opportunities to multiply our nestegg . . . and that's what this book is all about. The bad news is that, if you're not careful, you may not escape the poorhouse.

Part of the problem is that we're bewildered about money because it no longer works in the simple, old-fashioned way. Fixed-interest passbook savings have been traded in for wildly fluctuating money market accounts. We flounder in a world without stable reference points, where no matter how much we earn, we sense it isn't adequate for our needs. The old values of hard work, prudence, self-denial, and an occasional piece of luck along the way are no longer enough. For millions of Americans, habits about money die hard; they feel they've lost their grip on the present and that whatever is being done with money is strange and unsettling.

When I went to rent a car recently, there was a man ahead of me. "Do you have a major credit card?" The man shook his head and held out a wad of twenty dollar bills. "I'm sorry," the smiling young woman said. "Company policy forbids renting cars to anyone without a major credit card." By now the man in front of me was furious, waving cash in the air to prove he was rich, but she, a creature of the eighties, was not going to rent him a car even if he put up the deed to the Empire State Building as a deposit. He knew it.

Money has become something we save in the abstract—balances on a computer tape and numbers on a bank statement. We never expect to spend it or handle it; we write checks and use our credit cards. "Imagine thinking he could rent a car without a major credit card," this creature of corporate decree informed me. "It's people like that who are always disrupting the system."

Like renting a car, it's important to recognize how the financial marketplace has changed, how it will operate in the future. Deregulation boils down to this: Financial institutions are in a gloves-off competition for the saver's dollar. Congress will radically expand the IRAs to help save the nation's retirement system and Social Security. Saving money will be different and more complicated as all financial institutions begin to look alike, but it will be more rewarding.

The moral of this book: If you're anxious to save a buck and save on the higher taxes that are sure to come, now is the time to start looking for ways to beat the system. I hope you're as eager as I am to flip the page and get started learning how to stay ahead in the money game.

2

BANKS AND THRIFTS:
THE CHANGING WAY TO SAVE

No longer content to deposit their savings at a bank, most Americans keep the smallest possible balance in their checking accounts and move their money from one financial institution to another in search of the best deal. And, as financial deregulation spreads, where to find the best deal is fast becoming the highlight of carpool conversation.

The Reagan administration, the U.S. Treasury, and the Federal Reserve Board believe the big financial institutions need more freedom to compete with the money supermarkets. Their plan would draw new boundaries within the financial services industry by allowing banks and thrifts to compete head-on with other financial companies.

Specifically, Congress is being asked to allow bank and thrift holding companies or their subsidiaries to underwrite and make a market in U.S. government and municipal revenue bonds, to sponsor and sell mutual funds, insurance, and real estate, and to engage in securities brokerage transactions.

But allowing banks and thrifts to expand into other financial services raises a thorny question about the whole regulatory mechanism . . . about deposit insurance. In the seemingly irresistible rush toward deregulation, Congress has, in effect, already been bypassed, like trying to lead a parade from behind.

The parade started on the outskirts of a small windblown prairie city, 1,400 miles from New York and 1,800 miles from Los Angeles. There sits Citibank, a massive protest against the antiquated banking laws we discussed in the last chapter, in the middle of nowhere, some might think. But it's a godsend to the people of Sioux Falls, South Dakota, who attracted Citibank in 1980 in a dispute between banks and New York State over the 12% New York interest rate ceiling on consumer credit. South Dakota Governor William Janklow promptly went after the 1,500 jobs that Citibank dangled in front of him if his state could come up with what the bank wanted most: the lifting of the interest rate ceiling on credit cards.

Janklow knew the mathematics: fifteen hundred white collar jobs in a state badly shaken by recent defections to the Sun Belt. There would be a political windfall of major proportions. The state legislature quickly removed most interest rate ceilings entirely, and then it invited the New York-based bank into the state. Almost overnight a massive, slab-shaped modernistic building sprang up near a truck stop and a mobile home dealership to become home to over eight million Citibank credit card customers.

What Citicorp started in Sioux Falls has now been happening here and there all over the economic landscape as the nation's financial services continue to pry open loopholes in the banking laws and reach out to hire more people to help with the burgeoning money-handling and paperwork chores. As it turns out, the money-handling business has already overtaken the traditional smokestack economy. From 1973 to 1982, the Bureau of Labor Statistics estimated the number of jobs in finance, insurance, and real estate rose 32% to 5.4 million, while jobs in metal working, autos, and textiles were declining 38% to 2.4 million. During this period, jobs in banking and credit surged 40% to 2.2 million.

The size of the financial paper-working industry has not been well publicized because it has grown gradually. For example, since the end of World War II, the number of branch banks has increased from four thousand to more than forty-three thousand. At the same time, individual financial assets have soared about nineteen times to a total of $230 billion. The bottom line is this: with real income rising year after year, many American families for the first time have discovered they have a nest egg to conserve and manage.

With banking and saving decontrols spreading like wildfire, and advances in telecommunications allowing paperwork operations to be moved almost anywhere, the financial services boom began to pick up steam in the early 1980s. By 1982 banks were no longer banks, brokers were no longer brokers, and the Glass-Steagall Act of 1933 had been neatly sidestepped in the headlong chase for the consumer's dollar. "Financial Supermarkets" became the fashion. The goal was to offer a wide range of financial services under one roof.

And then, in the closest thing yet to breaching the wall between the solid, safe world of banking and the perilous business of buying and selling stocks, Bank of America got federal permission in 1983 to buy the largest discount stockbrokerage house in America, Charles Schwab and Company. With fifty-one offices across the country, Schwab now had a chance to open discount brokerage offices in more than one thousand branches of the bank.

The world of discount brokers dawned in 1975 when the Securities and Exchange Commission mandated the end of fixed commissions on the sale and purchase of stocks and bonds. This new deregulation, it turned out, allowed anyone to set up shop and buy or sell securities to their customers. Small, regional discount brokers began to spring up, but it was not until 1981 that banks and thrifts started to take a serious look at the brokerage business.

What made possible the banks' and thrifts' entry into the brokerage business was the discovery that Schwab was not a full-service brokerage firm. The Glass-Steagall Act, Bank of America argued, prohibits banking institutions from underwriting or promoting securities, on the theory that consumers' deposits should not be vulnerable to the whims of Wall Street. Since Schwab merely processed buy-and-sell orders, did not give advice or provide securities research, or recommend particular stocks, it was therefore not a securities firm, in the eyes of the law.

"I think this [deal] would have been legal ten years ago," says Steve McLin, Bank of America's director of strategic planning. "But nobody figured it out. We want to get about as close to Glass-Steagall as we can without breaking the law." For example, Bank of America wants to offer its customers something previously reserved for full-service brokerage houses—new stock issues. If the bank did not guarantee the sale of the new issue, the bank believes it would not technically be underwriting, and the bank's customers could, for the first time, buy new securities when they are issued.

Once the Schwab merger with Bank of America was approved, banks and thrifts began to move into the discount brokerage business in a big way, offering their customers an almost unlimited choice of securities trading for their own accounts. For full-service brokers, the new discount brokerage business was a life-threatening move into the heart of the securities business. Banks and thrifts, with cut-rate prices and low overhead, could easily take over the consumer end of the business. As one broker for a full-service house said, "Now that we have competition, it will be impossible to unscramble the egg."

But for big banks like Citibank, whose parent, Citicorp, owns its own satellite communication system with four earth-receiving stations (including one at Sioux Falls), unlimited credit card interest and discount brokerage business were now small potatoes. The gravy was in insurance.

Citicorp wanted a new *state* law that would allow state-chartered banks to sell insurance. This would be the crack they needed to skirt the federal law barring national banks from the insurance business.

The state of Delaware rushed to make its insurance laws more lenient, to attract the banking giant. Delaware had already won eighteen hundred new bank jobs by abolishing interest ceilings and offering a sliding-scale tax on bank profits. Among the dozen new bank offices in the state were those of New York's five biggest banking institutions.

But South Dakota was not asleep. The state legislature immediately grasped the point that Citicorp was again shopping for the best deal and erased state laws that would bar the bank from giving them the high-paying, white-collar jobs that fit so well in the depressed prairie state.

About half-a-dozen states in recent years have passed laws that allow state banks to pursue businesses that federal law prohibits, but South Dakota had clearly come out the winner. "We've been moving very rapidly," said a Citicorp spokesman. "We're buying a bank in South Dakota." The bank, tiny American State Bank of Rapid City, had total assets of just $15 million, versus Citicorp's $130 billion. After the purchase, a Citicorp lawyer smiled, "It's like trying to drive a camel through the needle's eye. Sometimes the cracks in the law are so small, only dwarf banks can get through. After all," he went on, "the purpose of the federal system is to let states experiment. Nevada did it with divorce law, Delaware did it with corporate law. Now South Dakota's done it with insurance law."

Once Citicorp establishes an insurance base, or it simply buys one of the major insurance companies, the bank can sell insurance nationally, if it obtains licenses from individual insurance authorities. "Then," said one banker, "when we make a loan on a car, truck, or piece of equipment, we won't have to send the customers down the street to get the insurance before we can complete the loan. We can just ask them to step over to the insurance counter, and we can wrap up the deal in a few minutes."

The new law letting South Dakota banks into the insurance business—forbidden territory for national banks—quickly attracted a second major national banking giant, First Interstate Bancorp, of Los Angeles. They agreed to buy tiny Big Stone State Bank in Big Stone City because, as a spokesman for First Interstate said, "It was available, and all we really wanted was the damn charter, anyway."

The banks' and thrifts' assault on the insurance business, once they gear up their marketing program, will be vicious. Selling insurance has always meant fat profit margins, but the float on the money collected as premiums could make bankers fall on their knees in front of a reluctant insurance buyer. "Hell," one thrift executive told me, "why go for depositors who can yank the cash out when you least expect it. If I can pile up the kind of float we're talking about by selling insurance," he said, "I would be top dog in the company. Beautiful women would cross strange rooms just to inhale my after-shave lotion," he grinned.

With insurance already being sold at Sears, J. C. Penney, and Kroger food stores, banks and savings and loans want the same ability to package a full line of insurance and meet the competition from their nonbank rivals. To get a jump on the wave of financial deregulation, some insurance companies are leasing space in bank lobbies as a way to sell insurance cheaply. The time-honored method of selling homeowner and auto insurance through insurance agents has become costly and inefficient. Banks point out that many "agency" companies spend thirty cents or more of every first-year premium dollar on sales costs, which are rising.

Thrift institutions, stripped of a big chunk of their assets by the more aggressive nonbanks—like brokerage firms and mutual funds—are turning from patsy to killer. Groups of savings and loans around the country have joined together to compete with major banks for multimillion-dollar corporate loans. And faced with less restrictive legislation than banks, the S&Ls are already offering their customers discount brokerage services, mutual funds, and car, home, and life insurance.

"Savings and loans," my friend told me, "that's where I used to go to get a mortgage to buy a house; now they want to loan me money to buy a car or truck. They want to give me six years to pay for the car. So what do they do? They even offer to loan me money for a used car!" He shakes his head because he doesn't understand the rules anymore.

In California, Sears wants to move its Sears Financial Network into the local branches of its statewide Allstate Savings and Loan, turning them into one-stop financial supermarkets. Allstate's lobby would include a savings and loan, Dean Witter Reynolds (investment securities), Coldwell Banker (real estate), and Allstate (auto, fire, and life insurance). A Sears executive told me, "A customer can buy a home, arrange for the mortgage, insure the property, get a loan for a car, invest in or sell stocks and bonds . . . all at the same place the weekly paycheck is cashed."

What does all this change mean to you and me? How can you cope with the news that your banker is your broker? How can you talk about money and avoid stupid conversations among your friends? The answer: Understand just what each financial institution can do for you and when to use its services. The problem with this advice is that it will require you to change the way you think about money. You will have to realize that financial institutions, spurred on by profit incentives that made America great, are not always after your best interest. They want your money at the lowest cost at which they can attract it, and they want to lock it up for as long as they can.

Why do you think there's $200 billion of savings account money, more than all the money market funds combined, still sitting in the banks at 5.25% interest? The answer is trust . . . with a big capital T. Millions of people in this country continue to believe in banks and in the safety of a bank account. Their parents kept their money there, so did their grandparents . . . and so they feel secure. Confused in a world of financial deregulation, they are reluctant to move, even when scores of savings plans, covered by federal insurance, offer them almost twice the interest on their money. They are still living with the Great Depression.

But we must get out of the thirties. The reason you're reading this book is to find out how to play the money game in the eighties. It is not my purpose to advise you on where you should save or invest. After all, I don't know anything about your income, assets, tax bracket, and long-range financial goal. What I can do is help you look behind the sixty-second television commercials about money so that even if the rules keep changing, you can stay ahead in the money game.

Let's take a look at some of the products and services offered by banks and thrifts . . . and how you can keep from being ripped off when you confront the established money grabbers with your hard-earned paycheck.

Insurance Protection

Today you have two agencies that protect your deposits up to $100,000 for each account. The Federal Savings and Loan Insurance Corporation protects the thrifts. The Federal Deposit Insurance Corporation protects the banks. For over fifty years these insurance agencies have worked well, protecting every saving account against the possibility of loss. But now the government wants to make a sweeping overhaul of the federal system of insuring banks and thrifts. Part of the problem is the misuse of the federal insurance (which we'll get into later), and part of the problem is the confusion resulting from the financial deregulation sweeping the nation.

What the regulatory agencies—the Federal Reserve Board, the comptroller of the currency, and the Federal Home Loan Board— would like to do is peg the price the bank or thrift pays for deposit insurance to the condition of its own balance sheet. The idea "in the absence of rigid government controls on competition, is to limit destructive competition and excessive risk taking." In other words, if a bank or thrift fails in the no-holds-barred competitive market, the burden of paying off the customers should not continue to come entirely out of the insurance fund.

The idea is for banks to be classified as either high-risk, medium-risk, or normal, according to how prudently they are run. The higher the risk, the higher the deposit-insurance premiums. The FDIC now believes that at least 10% of all U.S. banks are currently high risks, about 10% medium risks. But what has the bankers' teeth chattering is the threat by the FDIC "to encourage them [the banks] to behave more cautiously" by making public each bank's classification.

Services and Fees

Deregulation has made bank and thrift profit margins paper thin, requiring these institutions to take another look at the services they previously provided at little or no cost. As one banker put it, "You're going to see new, higher, and more imaginative checking service charges and fees attached to the accounts at many banks. For many customers who stop and think about it, and fortunately for us most don't, the charges will greatly reduce effective interest yields on their demand deposits." Waxing enthusiastic at the idea of explicit pricing, he went on. "Now that we're paying more for our money, you'll see us charge for every service we provide."

"Including waiting on people in your bank?" I asked.

"Hell, yes," he said. "In fact, Citibank tried to make depositors with less than $5,000 in their account use the new automatic teller machines, stay out of bank lines altogether. But the public outrage was so great that they've gone back to waiting on people again. It's only a matter of time before rules like that will become the way all banks operate."

"The old saw about the customer being king is not true?" I asked.

"No. The small depositor's crown fell off last year. Now if the little customer wants to put in or take out money, there is the branch's electronic banking machine. A machine costs us a third of what a human teller costs us. It's the small depositor's transaction business that's the unprofitable bummer. In the long run, banks offering the most service now will either stick on hefty charges for everything . . . or go broke."

Of all the institutions we deal with, banks and thrifts are the most imperious. If it weren't for the profits they can make on our money, they wouldn't have anything to do with us at all. For years the lines in front of the tellers' windows in most big city banks have been long enough to make me think of robbery rather than withdrawal. In my bank, I know for certain they have more "next window please" signs than they have tellers. Paying a teller costs a bank more money than installing a machine, but I'm not sure the average American is as ready for computerized money as the banks are.

Most banks are already disregarding their customers' convenience—and their pocketbooks. They confound savers by luring them with big bonuses on one account one month and then whacking them with fees on another the next. Most banks and thrifts operate with nothing in mind but their own convenience and profit, because small savers and investors—people like you and me—no longer pay their way in the expensive world of big-time banking.

Ultimately, many of us with a small bucket of cash are going to bear the brunt of the higher fees as banks and thrifts try to recoup their losses by charging the average depositor and saver more. As the rules continue to change, we'll have to calculate how much money we regularly keep on deposit and how many checks we write each month. We may have to deal with cold, passionless machines in our grocery store or shopping mall. We may rarely step inside a bank or thrift as the cost of helping the small depositor soars . . . unless our banker is our broker.

Discount Brokerage

Each weekday afternoon Jack Thompson walks up to a computer display terminal at his local savings and loan office to check the prices of his stocks. Mesmerized by the green flashing prices dancing along the face of the cathode ray tube quote machine, he smiles as his stocks continue to ride the roaring market. Next to the terminal is a direct-line telephone for him to buy and sell his leaping stocks—transactions that can be automatically settled as credits or debits in his checking account.

Ajax paper cups is about to make a break out of its trading range, a leap to a higher price. Jack's been following the stock for the last three weeks, and it's been building a steadily rising volume and price. He buys one hundred shares at $55, a transaction that typically would have cost him $92 at a full-service broker. He'll pay only $45 at his favorite savings and loan.

What Do Discount Brokers Do?

They don't offer you a strategy for a lifetime of investment opportunity and financial security. They won't help you cope with a financial world that has become infinitely more complex. Unlike the full-service brokers who ask you to "bring us your future," their main job is simply to sell you stocks and bonds you already know you want to buy or sell.

If you, like Jack Thompson, step into a bank or thrift and call the discount broker, you will talk with an employee—the next available one—who will act as your agent in buying or selling securities. For acting as your agent in the sale or purchase of securities, discount brokers charge a fee anywhere from 50% to 70% less than you would pay to a full-service broker. Discount brokers can execute your transaction on all national and regional exchanges, and dive into the "pink sheets" to execute your trades in the over-the-counter market. Like full-service brokers, they have Securities Investor Protection Corporation (SPIC) insurance, which protects customers against the firm's liquidation for up to $500,000 (up to $100,000 for claims in cash).

Once you hold securities in your name, discount brokers can offer you the same services as full-service brokers: free safekeeping accounts; periodic statements with all transactions, including dividends; automatic transfers to your checking account; and cash management to keep your idle cash at work.

What Discount Brokers Don't Do

By law they can't as yet underwrite new issues, hold stock in their own name, or ask you to buy a particular stock or bond. To keep costs low, discount brokers do not offer investment advice or research and advisory services to their customers. To cut costs even further, discount brokers employ no salespeople; their registered brokers are compensated by salary. Because many of the larger discount brokers are owned by banks and thrifts, they provide full-margin services (you buy securities with a down payment and borrow the balance from the broker) at interest rates that are among the industry's lowest.

What Services Do They Offer?

Discount brokers, as they begin to operate inside the offices of their parent banks or thrifts, will continue to expand their services. Most will offer you credit cards and checking accounts. They will be able to sell money-market accounts, no-load mutual funds, and tax-free bonds, and many of them now offer their own cash-management account. The usual amount to open an account is $1,000 in cash or $5,000 in securities.

Who Should Use a Discount Broker?

Since discount brokers have no commissioned salesperson to give you help or advice with your security portfolio, do not ask for—or expect to receive—investment advice or help. The discount broker is acting only as your agent in the transaction and cannot give you any information that you might use to purchase or sell stocks or bonds. Saving 50% to 70% of the full-service brokerage fee is not a bargain if you're not sure what or when you should buy or sell your stocks or bonds.

Where Can You Find a Discount Broker?

At almost any bank or thrift. The big banks have the largest discount brokers. (Bank of America owns Charles Schwab, and Chase Manhattan Bank bought out Rose and Company.) But this is small potatoes compared to the mergers now in the works.

As the legal wall between bankers and brokers continues to crumble, a world is being created in which Morgan Stanley and Morgan Guaranty might emerge as the House of Morgan, or Citicorp itself might become bullish on Merrill Lynch. What banks and thrifts are really after is a way to make money—through lucrative fees—without the credit risk that making more loans would bring to their balance sheets. There must be at least a thousand banks and thrifts offering discount brokerage service, with the number to rise sharply in the coming months.

Banks and thrifts are not alone in eyeballing the profitable discount brokerage business. New England Life's agents will offer discount brokerage through a unit of Fidelity Brokerage Services, which is a part of the Fidelity Group, a Boston-based financial services concern. A spokesman for the big life insurer believes that current customers for life insurance will choose to trade securities through New England Mutual because they know and trust its agents. The insurance company already has an investment counseling firm, seven mutual funds, and a large annuity operation.

New England Mutual's entry into the discount brokerage business is another example of the way financial deregulation has broken away from the brick and mortar. The pace of change has dropped the entry price to the banking, savings, and securities business so low that New England Mutual believes it can save the expense of buying an established firm and spend only $275,000 in start-up costs and about $200,000 in advertising. At these prices, you can expect a surge of insurance companies and mutual funds jumping into the discount brokerage market. To get a better idea of the new saving and checking plans, let's take a look at what the money-grabbers are offering in those splashy full-page ads. With deregulation, it's like every day is a month-end sale.

Money-Market Checking

Those unlimited-interest paying Super-Checking accounts (Super-NOW) come with higher, more imaginative service charges than ever before. So much so that many bankers believe it's entirely possible that customers will earn only marginally more than the 5.25% they already receive on NOW accounts—maybe even less.

Previously, banks and thrifts were limited to offering zero-interest regular checking accounts or negotiable order of withdrawal (NOW) accounts paying 5.25% on the surplus cash sitting in the checking account from month to month. With the lifting of interest rate limitations, Super-NOW unlimited-interest-bearing checking accounts have burst on the scene, pushing banks and thrifts into offering what amounts to a combined saving/checking account. Known in some states as "Super-checking," the Super-NOW accounts usually allow unlimited checks and unlimited interest rates. Theoretically, that sounds like a good deal. But banks and thrifts must set aside reserves equal to 12% of deposits collected in the new accounts. That means that twelve cents out of every dollar in deposits will not be available for making loans—or, from the bank's point of view, for each dollar on deposit on which interest is paid, only eighty-eight cents can be loaned out again.

The Federal Reserve Board estimates that it costs the average bank or S&L about $3.35 a month to maintain a checking account, about thirteen cents to process each check, and about twenty-seven cents to process each deposit. These costs are slightly higher for Super-NOW accounts because of the interest calculations, but the higher costs, coupled with the higher interest rates for Super-NOWs, have to be passed on to the consumer. In order to recover these higher costs, banks and thrifts have launched slick advertising campaigns to make the Super-NOWs look competitive, yet they are imposing hefty maintenance, penalties, and service fees.

"People have a vague idea that if you have $2,500 you can get a hell of lot better rate than you are getting now," a bank officer explained, "but they don't know much more. What they don't know," he went on, "is that we were afraid we'd lose a lot of money if consumers transferred their money from zero-interest checking accounts to high-interest checking, so we loaded the new Super-NOWs with service charges, penalties, and clauses that drastically cut back the actual interest earned in these new accounts." To give you a better look at just where checking accounts stand today, here's the lineup of available choice.

Regular Zero-Interest Checking Account

This account can be opened for a minimum balance and you can pay for each check and/or you can pay a monthly service charge of between $2.50 and $4.50. This is by far the most popular checking account since millions of Americans have learned to keep just enough cash in their account to cover their outstanding checks. For most savers, it also happens to be the lowest cost way of paying their bills.

NOW Checking Account

These accounts can usually be opened for $1,000 or $1,500, and when these minimum balances are maintained a service charge may not apply. Some accounts charge ten or fifteen cents a check, and in a few cases, service charges are higher than a regular zero-interest account. Your account should earn 5.25% interest on the minimum balance, less the service charges, and to sweep you off your feet, many NOW accounts provide free printed checks as part of the package.

Super-NOW Checking Accounts

The minimum balance is $2,500, however, you'll have to plan on a balance of at least $3,500 to $5,000 if you're going to make Super-NOW work to your advantage.

You'll need a big balance because you'll be charged a monthly service fee, anywhere from $5 to $10, as part of the Super-NOW package. In some cases, if you maintain a high minimum balance, $5,000—or as high as $10,000—in your account, you can earn a half-point to three-quarters point more interest on your money. In many Super-NOW accounts, you'll also be asked to pay fifteen to twenty cents for each check processed.

Why are Super-NOW checking accounts such a bad deal? Basically, because they are a bad deal for the financial institution, brought on by deregulation, which has come faster than the industry anticipated—and with it much higher costs than anyone expected. For example, look closely at the fine print. On a minimum balance of $2,500, a $6-a-month service fee is the same as 3% interest on your money. If the Super-NOW checking account is offering a "high" interest rate of 8% with a $6-a-month fee, your net interest is only 5% . . . less than the old NOW account, which pays 5.25%. But the most imaginative charge may be the kicker in your contract when your account balance falls below the minimum of $2,500 (and most bankers believe these accounts frequently will). Your earned interest for that statement period could fall to 5.25%, with a net interest after the service charges and penalty fees of about 2.25%.

Super-Checking can be summed up best by the comments of a banker for a large state-wide bank in California. "The fees will make Super-Checking unattractive for about 80% of our customers. They just don't have enough money," he explained. Privately, bankers tell me that people who write lots of checks (more than an average of twenty-two a month) and who don't keep several thousand dollars in their checking account, are unlikely to gain with Super-Checking. On the other hand, tying up large chunks of cash in a checking account with the high interest rates available today to make Super-Checking work is not good cash management.

How can you avoid the stiff fees on high-yield checking accounts? Not by reading the fine print in the advertisements when they appear on your TV screen or in the newspapers. The competition to attract your dollar has forced the fine print to gradually disappear. If you're in doubt, ask your financial institution the following questions:

● How much is the monthly service charge? (Remember, for every $1-a-month in fees, you're losing .5% of interest on $2,500.)

● How do they calculate their interest rate when your account balance falls below $2,500? (The worst way is to penalize you for the entire statement period by giving you only 5.25% if your balance falls below the minimum for even one day. The best way is to count only those days your balance dips below the minim at 5.25%.)

● Do they charge a penalty fee every time the account falls below the minimum of $2,500? (That is, will you get the lower interest rate of 5.25% *and* a penalty fee if your balance slides below the minimum of $2,500.)

• Do they have a charge for processing each check? (The cost could run you between twelve and twenty cents for each check!)

• Can the monthly service fee jump from, say, $6 up to $10 when the balance falls below $2,500? One of the most attractive ways they add profits to their operations is to slide in the service charges. At first glance, they don't look important. They only apply under certain conditions, which the bank or thrift assures you will not be a problem with your *method of saving*. But don't overlook the service charges; they can apply frequently, and they can be costly.

As far as I'm concerned, the high-interest-paying Super-Checking accounts have turned out to be something less than super. I keep most of my check writing money in a old-fashioned, regular noninterest-paying checking account—and then keep only enough money in the bank to cover my outstanding checks. I feel I can manage my money as well as the banks and thrifts, without their stiff service fees.

Passbook Accounts

With financial deregulation screaming in our ears, with banks and thrifts permitted to pay whatever rates they choose, the least attractive method of saving is the old relic of the past, the passbook accounts. They pay 5.25%, are protected by federal insurance, and you can withdraw the money at any time.

More than $2 billion continues to rest in these accounts—more money than the high-flying, aggressive, money market mutual funds have been able to attract in their twenty-some year history!

For many Americans, financial deregulation has come too late. Escaping from the Great Depression, they are now captives of an insidious television and newspaper campaign designed to keep their money where it will do the financial institutions the most good. You may have seen the television commercial in which a retired old codger, walking along a garden path, is trying to explain to an exasperated young man why he is content to let his money rest safely in his old passbook savings account, rather than step out in pursuit of higher earnings and risk losing it all.

The message you hear: I can't take any risks, not even moving my insured account within the financial institution and practically doubling my interest income, *because change means risk*. Though my own credentials as a money expert are not without some question, I can still remember the chapter in the Bible in which Jesus chased the moneychangers from the steps of the temple. It has caused me to wonder if we don't have the moneychangers operating today in reverse, keeping the money locked up for their own profit and greed, creating doubt and distrust in people who seek to take advantage of the expanding savings market while retaining whatever safety gives them peace of mind.

If you are still trapped in the passbook mentality, I hope I can lead you out to the fresh winds of change to give you confidence that changes in the way you save need not affect the safety of your funds. Many of the new ideas for saving and investing money won't turn a Pac-man loose on your pocketbook.

Now let's get beyond the passbook savings accounts and look at what choices we really have.

Certificates of Deposits

Certificates of deposits are another new savings idea as financial deregulation rolls along and crowds newspapers and television with more savings plans. One savings and loan's advertisement came right to the point. A would-be saver exclaims, "I'm so confused with all these savings plans that I'm going to put my money under the mattress and forget about the whole thing." And to add to our confusion, the banks and savings & loans can now strip away more regulations, offer higher interest rates, and lower the minimum deposits for this new set of fixed-term savings accounts.

Under financial deregulation, the old variety of four or five certificates of deposit (CDs) has given way to a single new account with which you can choose a fixed term of anywhere from thirty-two days to ten years. With this new flexibility, banks and thrifts will begin to market "designer" CDs that let a customer establish their duration. You could choose, for example, a 154-day certificate to mature when a college tuition payment is due, or a 240-day certificate when your property tax is due. If you later decide that you need the money before your CD matures, the new regulations make it easier to get your hands on the cash. For certificates maturing in a year or less, the withdrawal penalty is cut from three month's interest to one. For CDs of longer than a year, the penalty is cut in half, to three months' interest.

Banks and S&Ls will be able to pay whatever interest rate they want and to compound interest in any fashion, giving you the opportunity to shop for the best rates of interest on these new term accounts. Out-of-state banks and thrifts, using their toll-free numbers and the mail, will begin to market these new CDs aggressively, often paying higher interest rates to attract your money across state lines. As a result, you'll have to be savvy to take advantage of the new regulations. You'll have to shop carefully and read the fine print since financial institutions will be offering lots of different deals, with varying interest rates and maturities, and you'll have a tough time making comparisons.

Money Market Accounts

Money market accounts differ from fixed-term certificates of deposit in two basic ways. First, you can withdraw your money at any time without an interest penalty since money market accounts have no fixed term of deposit. And second, the minimum deposit to open a money market account is $2,500, while the minimum for a CD fixed-term account can be as low as $100.

When money market accounts burst on the scene, the ads signaled "The first major change in saving plans in a generation. Now you can earn unlimited interest on your savings, with federal insurance protection." Money market accounts were brought to you by the people at your local bank, and savings and loan, as their opening salvo in the new unregulated war with their archenemy, the mutual funds and stockbrokers.

When the new money market accounts began in December of 1982, they offered the best rates around—in some cases, a 20% or 25% annual return. That lured a lot of customers. Unfortunately, the fine print never made its way into the ads: The banks and thrifts could change the rate of interest they pay on a daily basis. And they did. By March 1983, when the bloom was off the accounts, the rates plunged to 8%, about equal with money market mutual funds.

But by trying to remain competitive with surging money market funds, banks and thrifts have had to learn a painful lesson. They now saw their deposits rushing out of their low-cost savings accounts into their high-priced money market accounts. Many small country banks, with as much as 40% to 50% of their deposits in low-cost savings plans, refused to offer the new accounts. A small-town banker who turned up his nose at the new money market accounts said, "Our deposits are holding right in there. I believe most of our customers are more interested in the quick personal service the bank provides than in the interest rates they earn on deposits." And this may be true.

For most big city banks and thrifts, however, it was a different story. They had been pleading with Congress to give them an account in which they could compete with the mutual funds and brokers. Originally they wanted a minimum of $5,000, making it more attractive for them to lust after the hard cash, but in the end they had to settle for a minimum of only $2,500. The money market account can be an excellent way to save short-term money if you fully understand its limitations and rules.

Like Super-Checking, you'll need to maintain at all times at least $2,500 in your account. If you fall below this level (your account then can earn the minimum passbook rate of 5.25%), the loss of interest can more than wipe out any gains you might otherwise achieve. You can be limited to six transactions a month, three by check and three by automatic transfer. Interest rates are not set by law; most financial institutions will reserve the right to change the interest rate on a daily basis. To give you the comfort of a bank or thrift, the money market accounts are insured by federal insurance up to $100,000 for each account.

In many cases, however, while appearing to promise you more, banks and thrifts are actually guaranteeing less. Banking regulations haven't yet been established for the free-wheeling, insured money market accounts. The government, in effect, lets them cheat. The SEC can and does keep money market mutual funds in line, checking their advertising with a magnifying glass before it's allowed to reach printer's ink. For example, you could be misled:

• When banks and savings and loans compare their "effective yields" with current interest paid by money-market funds. Banks and thrifts can advertise compound "effective yields," appearing to pay more, when both may have the same basic interest rate. Beware of an ad if it says it will pay more than an average seven or thirty-one day rate, unless you know the *simple* interest rate paid on the funds.

• When banks and thrifts advertise gross yield without deducting service charges or fees. The SEC requires mutual funds and brokers to substract all charges before publishing their rates, or to mark them up in bold-face type. Many times, sales commissions have been deducted from the interest rate shown in the advertisement.

● When banks and thrifts proclaim their $2,500 "low" minimum deposit required to open an account. Until the government established the new insured money-market accounts, $2,500 was a relatively large minimum deposit. Money funds start at $500, brokers at $1,000. And with these accounts you can write checks while you receive the full interest rate, no matter how low your balance may sink after you've established the account.

Money Market Rate Accounts

Sensing that the pace of financial deregulation is picking up faster than expected, some thrifts have moved away from FSLIC insurance and the structured savings accounts of the past. The bigs are pushing hardest, claiming that the rise of competition from nonbank "financial supermarkets" is catching them with hands tied. What they want is the flexibility to compete with money-market mutual funds and brokers . . . and to boost profits hurt by the explosive growth of nonbanks invading their turf.

The first of a growing number of savings packages is the Money Market Rate Account. Designed to compete with the money market mutual fund, this new savings plan offers a choice of four, eight, or twelve-week terms, a minimum deposit of only $1,000, and high rates that exceed the money market account with it's $2,500 minimum balance. The money you save is 100% secured by U.S. government-backed obligations held by a third-party trustee.

What's important to understand, in the fast-moving world of financial deregulation, is that the savings and loan is only *acting as a money middleman,* helping us invest in government debt. Your money is as safe as FSLIC-protected deposits, and these new accounts carry no interest penalty for early closing—just a $10 early redemption fee. The irony of financial deregulation is that banks and thrifts are spending millions to attract *and hold* savings deposits in their money market accounts and yet, at the same time, they are offering higher-paying market rate accounts without interest penalties and service charges.

Fixed-Term Savings

When you lend money for a fixed-term, you're gambling that you can outguess the financial institution on the future course of interest rates and inflation. Traditionally, the small investor or saver, which is to say the man or woman with a loose $5,000, $10,000, or so, has usually been in the wrong place at the wrong time. The unfortunate thing is that if you're right, you gain no more than the interest rate already promised in your long-term savings plan. If you're wrong, you continue to receive less than the market rate of interest, or you can withdraw your funds and face the old refrain, "a substantial interest penalty will be imposed for early withdrawals."

What most people don't realize is that locking up your savings for a fixed period is the same thing as buying a bond. The old rule of thumb I learned on Wall Street twenty years ago still applies: If interest rates go up, the value of your bond, or fixed-term savings, goes down. If interest rates go down, the value of your bond, or fixed-term savings, goes up. The problem, if you went into long-term savings as a safe harbor from the mad money market world, is that you can't come out a winner. If interest rates rise, as we've already said, you face a substantial loss to bail out and grab the higher return. If interest rates fall, you have no way to gain on your savings, if you went into bonds, falling interest rates work in your favor and the value of your investment increases to match the current market rates. Let's see how all of this works in the real world.

Suppose interest rates rise after you buy your bond. If, before maturity, you need to sell your 8-percent, $1,000 bond that yields you $80 per year, you won't be able to sell it for $1,000. Let's say the interest rate now available on bonds of the same grade as yours is 10%. It's hardly news that a buyer won't be interested in your $80-yield when he or she can get a $100 yield in a 10% market. A buyer will only be interested in your bond at a discount. The current market value of your 8% bond is now only $800, because that's a 10% return and no one is going to earn less than the going interest rate at the time of purchase. But if interest rates fall after you buy your bond, your investment will rise in value for the opposite reason. At least with a bond, you can make a profit if interest rates fall. You can't with a long-term savings account. We'll cover bonds more fully in the next chapter.

62

For long-term savings plans, interest can be computed from day of deposit to the maturity date. For some time deposit plans, the maturity date and the date that interest is paid are based on calendar quarters. The daily rate of interest for the money market accounts the cowboy on television asks you to buy to protect your hard-earned paycheck is usually calculated at 1/360 the annual interest rate. For all other time deposit plans, you should get daily interest calculated on 1/365 of the annual interest rate.

Fixed-term deposits usually range from three months up to ten years. The banks' and thrifts' ever-increasing appetite for locked-up cash provides you an almost unlimited choice of long-term savings plans. You can start off with three and six-month Treasury-Bill accounts, twelve, eighteen, thirty and forty-two-month time deposits, and for those who can see into the future beyond the next recession or recovery, up to ten years.

The rule of thumb when you lock up your money in a bank or thrift is: One, the larger your deposit, the higher the interest rate. For the heavy wallet crowd, $100,000 CDs will earn more than $5,000 market accounts for the same time deposit. And two, the longer you lock up your cash, the higher the interest rate.

If banks and thrifts are not your fancy, you can buy a T-Bill from the Federal Reserve or pay a sales commission and buy one from your local bank or thrift. Treasury-Bills are short-term obligations of the federal government. They are issued weekly and are payable in three or six months. T-Bills issued monthly are payable in one year. For more information or Treasury-Bills, see chapter 8.

The interesting thing about T-Bills is that they are sold at discount; that is, at a price below the face value of the bill with the difference between the face value and the purchase price representing the interest. Since they are exempt from state and local income taxes, their net yield can often exceed that of a bank or thrift saving plan. Treasury-Notes are issued at par, not at a discount, for two to ten years. They pay interest every six months. Bonds are issued for a minimum of ten years.

My advice to you is *never lock up your money longer then six months,* and never gamble against the market by imagining that you have just locked up the highest rate of all time. If you want to go "long-term," buy bonds or stocks with which you have a high degree of instant liquidity and can protect yourself when the investment goes sour.

Don't be surprised if your stockbroker asks you to invest in the stock of a savings and loan. Banks and thrifts, not content to wait for the money to come in the front door, want to purchase your money aggressively. It's not a bad deal for the brokers, either. On many stock sales, they get a fifty-cent bonus for every share of stock they get a customer to buy. In one month in 1983, three large savings and loans in California were selling nearly $700 million in stock. In New York, The Bowery Savings Bank purchased money by offering a cool $100 million of mortgage-backed bonds, paying 10⅞% due April 15, 1988.

How Will Banks and Savings and Loans Change?

Get ready for a wild and woolly roller coaster ride as the nation's thrifts discover that, like banks, they can purchase money and expand their loan portfolios. In fact, in a money world gone crazy with financial deregulation, all but the largest financial institutions are finding, in a money world gone crazy with financial deregulation, that they can no longer make all their profits on the "spread"—the difference between what they pay for money and what they can earn when they loan it out.

What you're going to see in the decade of the eighties is a major shift by most banks and thrifts away from their traditional role as money gatherers. Stephen McLin, senior vice president of big Bank of America, may have summed it up best when he said, "There may be no banks at all within the next few years. Not that they will all fail, but there will be such a blurring of distinctions among savings and loans, banks, brokerage houses, and other companies such as Sears and American Express, that some creative person will have to coin a new word for banks."

The new technology that is changing the banking world has already happened in the gas station business. The number of gas stations in the United States has fallen by one-third since the Arab oil embargo, yet they pump all the gas Americans want to buy. They used to provide an excess of convenience—what is now known as "full service"—which it turns out was not necessary. To stay competitive, gas stations moved to self-service in order to hold down labor costs. Banks and thrifts moved to automated teller machines to cut costs. Even the swiftest human teller cannot compete with a machine.

Most banks and savings and loans, while they may be profitable now, are an endangered species. To survive, they will become "middlemen," selling money products and making an increasing percentage of their profits on the hefty sales commissions they earn.

Already you see savings and loans, for example, selling stocks and bonds with their discount brokerage services, insurance on your life or home, tax-free bonds, and mutual funds. Even the new CD savings accounts are rapidly becoming something the thrift industry will be forced to *buy* rather than *sell* to the public. By letting brokers and money supermarkets sell the CDs to the public, thrifts can acquire them from these financial institutions and find a way to gain deposits that would otherwise not come in the front door.

With financial deregulation, brokers can now invade banks' and thrifts' turf, and Merrill Lynch is a good example of how brokers can beat the traditional money gatherers at their own game.

The broker will offer both short-term six-month CD Participations, with a choice of fixed rates or variable rates that change monthly and are said to be higher than Donoghue's Money-Fund Average of over 200 money funds. Or longer-term CDs from two-and-a-half to ten years. Merrill Lynch will also offer Zero Coupon CDs for IRAs and Keogh plans. Here's how the broker's CD plan will work:

The broker will shop the market, select the highest rate from a wide range of banks' and thrifts' CDs, and then use their Federal Deposit Insurance for its own CDs. The admission ticket here is $1,000 for the regular CDs and as little as $250 for the Zero Coupon CDs. Not only can you get the highest rate offered at the time you buy your CD, but brokers are going one step further. They are going to establish an active secondary market—a market where both short-term and longer-term CDs can be bought or sold at prevailing market prices so you can get your hands on the cash if you need your money before maturity. The secondary market can help you avoid the interest penalty typically associated with banks' and thrifts' early redemption policies and let you buy almost any maturity you need as your savings plans change.

The answer to getting the best deal on your savings and checking accounts should be obvious by now. You'll have to shop carefully and read the fine print. As financial deregulation continues to spread, banks, thrifts, brokers, mutual funds, and insurance companies will offer a surprising number of different savings plans, with varying interest rates and maturities. One thing is certain, you're going to have to change your perception of banks, savings and loans, and brokers. You're going to have to look first at where you save. You may find out that it won't be the brick-and-mortar money palace your father used.

America's investors and savers are on the brink of a revolution in service and products—intriguing in some respects, wrenching in others.

3

BROKERS: ONLY THE STRONG CAN SURVIVE

As I walked down the highly polished floors, past the paint and garden tractors, I quickened my pace nearing the men's fashion department. Maybe a new pair of loafers and I'd be back in business. And maybe a tie or two. After all, you feel like an idiot if you don't take advantage of these shamefully low prices. I tried on several different pairs of loafers and glanced across the aisle. I blinked. Could that be an office of a prestigious Wall Street broker? Could it be located in a Sears department store, hard by the shoe department? I moved across the aisle. The signs were unmistakably those of Dean Witter, heralded by a splashy new advertising campaign that was intended to change my present blurred perception of stately old Wall Street brokers into a convenient, easy-to-approach money center. But this, I discovered, was only part of Sears' new Financial Network—a strategy designed to package a financial supermarket in a shopping center and offer you fantastic returns on investing and saving money. It's a winning appeal to greed, I thought, and Sears has taken advantage of financial deregulation to open the doors.

With the establishment of Sears Financial Network in 1982, middle-class America was at last going to have a chance to rub elbows with the stock market and zero-coupon bonds. Sears advertising proclaimed "The financial services your family needs most . . . together for the first time." The Sears Financial Network includes Allstate Insurance (life, auto, fire); Dean Witter Reynolds (stocks, bonds, mutual funds); Coldwell Banker (real estate); and, for now, in California, Allstate Savings (savings and loan).

With Sears selling its name in hard-hitting advertising like: "We started Sears Financial Network to help bring American working people the financial advice and services they need . . . in a setting they know and trust," the going was so good that the all-things-to-all-people financial services firm jumped into the national market. The message was clear: You've trusted us since 1886, so why not come to us to buy or sell a house. Or take out insurance. Or invest in the stock market. Or save with a savings and loan. Or buy our money market fund.

In fact, Sears is now considering acquiring banks and S&Ls in other states (currently they have an S&L in California) that would let Sears take deposits through its stores and allow it to hook into the burgeoning automated-teller network. Sears also wants to give homeowners a revolving credit line backed by home equity. Customers could write checks against their credit line and buy securities, even some of Sears new conventional mortgage-backed securities.

As a grand finale to its new Financial Network, Sears is planning to offer an even better deal than a fantastic return on your money: If you buy products from their money store, they will give you discounts on such Sears products as furniture, appliances, and other home products.

So the beat goes on across the country. Radical changes in where and how we save, invest, borrow money. But whom do we trust? The shop inside a Sears department store, our local bank, some 800 number that leads our money out of state? Will Americans do their financial business in retail stores that don't have massive investments in brick and mortar? If so, and if it now costs companies like Sears only a few thousand dollars to open a savings and loan and a major New York stock broker branch, how soon will we have a financial McDonald's blanketing America? I don't know. Nobody does. But my guess is that by 1985 all of the current Wall Street brokers who sell their products to the public will be part of an overall financial supermarket, with offices combined with insurance companies, banks, or savings and loans. With the Reagan administration oozing deregulation from every pore, rapid changes will continue. A tidal wave of mergers and one-stop money shopping will wash away the barriers that separate financial institutions today.

By going to the public, Wall Street brokers can overcome a major handicap: most Americans find them intimidating—the rows of offices, computers on every desk, green-lighted numbers flashing along big signs. If you stop to talk with one of these money-people, you'd swear they're having trouble with the English language. They grab up your hard-earned cash, touting a "money multiplier trust" (don't you just love that phrase?). Or, with the same zeal that the devil abhors holy water, they help you find the cash you need to invest in almond groves by suddenly realizing that the inflated value in your home is money in the bank. Appearing to be highly sophisticated money management firms, many brokers and financial planners have been preying on the avarice of the new property-rich middle class, legitimizing the second mortgage by making it available.

Brokers push home seconds because they are always looking for ways to find money. Not the kind of money you can use to take a vacation to Rome or buy a Mercedes, but the kind of money they can invest for you, or if they are especially lucky, trade in the market. Beware, the sharp marketing people in the nation's major brokerage houses are continually on the lookout for ways to free up your cash to put you into the market, to invest your money in their products, to generate the life-saving commissions that pay the bills. Some scream, some speak in soft, soothing voices. But each dangles the same bait: high returns on your money. Before you invest, consider where the money came from. If you're thinking of a longer-term investment, is it money you have left over and you can spare? If it's short-term, is it money you can get your hands on when you're most likely to need it? Or, is it the latest caper now being pushed by brokers and banks, whereby you borrow money from yourself to invest?

I, for one, am still worried about where people get the money to save or invest. If you borrow it from your home equity, be cautious. Maybe *afraid* is a better word. If you invest or save it in solid, safe, debt instruments, you're likely to pay more for the borrowed money than you can earn. If you invest it where the asterisk explains, "the estimated anticipated yield is based on past performance and which, in our opinion, while not guaranteed offers attractive potential," you could easily end up with a washout. Like tossing hundred dollar bills out the window. Everyone will get rich but you.

If you've decided to approach a broker, try to avoid some of the mistakes millions of Americans make in search of higher returns. First of all, don't be intimidated by a busy broker's office. Your first step should be to determine what your objectives are. Are you looking for high risk and big rewards, or are you more conservative with an eye out for the safety of your investments. Above all, pick an investment approach that's comfortable. You may be looking for bargains—the asset-rich, low-multiple, screaming-value-type stock. Or you may be attracted to higher-multiple, emerging-growth companies. (A multiple is a stock's price-earnings ratio; in other words, how many times the stock's earnings equal the sale price. Generally, the higher the multiple, the riskier the stock.)

And remember, above all else, no one stock has to be bought, no one investment has to be made. The market will always be there. If you don't fully understand where you're being asked to risk your hard-earned cash, if you don't feel your broker has tilted the odds in your favor, back off. There is always another stock and always another day.

If you walk in off the street, you'll be assigned the broker who has the floor duty that day. He or she may not be the best broker for you and your investment objectives, so shop around. Ask the receptionist the name of the broker who specializes in your area of interest. Find out a little about the broker, what are his or her financial objectives and market approach, when would they advise you to sell in a falling market. If you're not comfortable with investments in a stock market that jumps up and down, say so. The time you spend finding out if you're compatible with a broker's feel of the market could well be the best time you can spend in search of higher earnings and profits.

Next, don't overrate the knowledge and skill of your broker. Unless you have a particularly experienced and knowledgeable broker, one whom you've come to trust, check out the person's recommendations before you invest. Remember, brokerages are like other businesses, they have an inventory of stocks and bonds in the back room; they want to move this merchandise. If you're not careful, many brokers will be glad to take your money off your hands and sell what's in inventory. Find out why their recommendation is a better investment than what's available in the marketplace, why they are asking you to take a big bet that the stock or bond offers such attractive potential.

Once you've finally selected that paper-into-plastic-cup stock you believe will travel faster than the Dow Jones Averages and give you a shot at making really big money, don't panic if the stock doesn't rise on good news or stays up on bad. Usually the news was expected and has already been discounted. It may have been known when you bought the stock. The single most important factor in boosting the price of your stock—or the market—is the element of surprise. And that's beyond your control.

Don't buy anything on margin (that is, buying securities with a down payment) unless you fully understand the risks you're taking, and you have the spare cash to rescue your investments when the market turns against you. The old adage of Wall Street rings true in the deregulated market of the eighties: don't speculate unless you can make it a full-time job.

Don't fall for the biggest mistake of all: thinking you can buy at the bottom and sell at the top. Once you own the security, learn how to take your losses quickly and cleanly. Perfect a sense of timing on the sell side. There are no more sacred cows. The eternal truth for investors is to learn how to sell before you buy—that's what makes bottom-line winners. Sell the bad stock or bond and keep the good. With rare exception, stocks are high because they are good, and stocks are low because they are of doubtful value. Another age-old Wall Street truism is that you should never sell a stock in which you have a profit in order to protect one in which you have loss. One of the worst mistakes you can make is to hold on blindly and refuse to admit that your judgment has been wrong. In fact, in today's volatile market, I would suggest that you talk with your broker about placing "stop-loss orders" on your stocks and bonds so that if the market turns against you, you'll sell out before you ride the price down and get hurt.

As long as bear markets follow bull markets, stop-loss orders will continue to protect the profits of smart investors. Let's say your stock is now selling for $30 a share. You're concerned that you might miss the next market downturn you read about in the papers. You've heard from the unpleasant bears who continue to dispense dire prophecies. So you ask your broker to put in a stop-loss order at $27. If your stock hits $27 a share, your stop-loss order then becomes a market order and it will be executed as soon as a sale can be completed at the market price. What price you set your stop-loss order will depend on your experience with the stock and the profit margin you are trying to protect.

People who watch television know about Doan's Pills that take the pain out of your aching back and Anacin for people who want pain plucked from their heads. But few people have heard of Nasdaq. Nasdaq is not a painkiller; in fact, it's not widely known outside the stock market crowd, and there's no reason why you should be familiar with Nasdaq. What makes Nasdaq important is that it's the machine that tells your broker about the unlisted securities market, where almost half the daily market volume occurs. It's called over-the-counter from the days when unlisted stocks were literally sold over the brokers' counter.

The over-the-counter market, once considered a side-show in stock trading, is gaining new prominence. Technological changes have made it easier for your broker to do business in the unlisted securities market. With the Nasdaq quote machine, trading in unlisted securities during the last five years has soared 205%, compared with 128% on the New York Stock Exchange and 35% at the American Stock Exchange.

The National Association of Securities Dealers Automated Quotation system, or Nasdaq, began in 1971 when the over-the-counter market went from mimeograph machine to computer screen. Since then, advances in electronic trading, multiple market makers, low cost, and comparatively little paperwork have attracted many of the newer companies that could easily meet the requirements for listing on structured exchanges. If the drift toward totally automated trading continues, Nasdaq, which has eclipsed the AMEX, could challenge the Big Board as the most active major exchange. With eighty thousand quote machines in the United States and some seven thousand in Europe, Nasdaq has been defined as "A three thousand-mile trading floor without pillars or marble."

If you're serious about becoming an investor on the major stock exchanges, or if you want to plunge into the over-the-counter market, you've got to keep one eye out for what the industry considers the "normal trading pattern." Most stocks are bought or sold in round-lot trades—one hundred or more shares of one stock issue. If you're forced into odd-lot trading—less than one hundred shares—the market can be inactive at times and the price you pay for the stock can be higher than the regular round-lot trade, reflecting the trouble your broker faces in breaking apart round-lot trades. If you're forced into odd-lot trading, consider investing in mutual fund stock plans instead.

The answer to getting the best deal in the stock market, however, may be a better understanding of what your broker is up to. The broker's life has changed dramatically with the burgeoning number of saving and investment plans coming onto the market and the shift of investors back into saving plans where they can grab double-digit interest rates. In 1980, on average, only about 50% of a broker's commission income came from equities, compared with about 85% as late as the 1970s.

Today, the average broker's income from equities has slipped below 50%, with the larger percentage of a typical broker's income now coming from longer-term securities, such as tax shelters, bonds, and mutual funds. The message delivered in this story means that brokers will have to work harder and sell more products to make the same income in the years to come.

Considering the record-breaking performance of the Dow Jones averages, you're probably expecting your broker to be dancing in the street. Not so. He's walking along the sidewalk in the rain. First, he's no longer getting his share of the business. The big volume on the exchanges now goes to the institutional market— some say as much as 60 to 70% of all the business on the major exchanges. Second, the new wave of fixed-income securities and mutual funds has locked up a big share of his customers' trading money.

By directing their sales fire at individuals who are seeking long-term investing, securities firms are forcing brokers to work harder to keep one of their most prized possessions: trading accounts where customers continually buy and sell stocks. In the world of the masterful broker, it's not how many accounts you have, but how often you can trade those accounts that makes the difference between driving a Mercedes and a Pontiac.

For the branch manager, trading accounts are equally important because they often determine the branch's bottom line. The more trades, the higher the profits. Since brokerage firms (like oil companies, newspapers, drug stores) are in business to make a profit, trading of customers' securities has become inordinately important. They are the tail that wags the dog—especially with the new rush of discount brokers who aggressively offer to trade securities at 50 to 70% off full-service brokers' commission rates. Trading is regaining more importance in the life of your broker, and you should guard against "excessive" trading in your decisions on investing.

Investing in securities takes a lot of work, investigation, and study. Bernard Baruch had a simple rule: Before you buy any security, find out everything you can about the company, its management and competitors, and its earnings and possibilities for growth. If you can't do that, find out if your broker has made this search before touting the latest sure-fire investment and socking your money into the greatest paper/plastic cup ever invented. If your broker can't come up with the right answers, get out. Rest on the sidelines. Most good stockbrokers know that once the average person enters the market and becomes mesmerized with the flashing prices leaping to new highs, he or she will be blind to discipline and deaf to the voice of experience. In the excitement of the chase for higher profits, emotion will prevail, while good sense and diligent homework will be thrown to the winds.

Brokerage firms offer the following storehouse of services and investments: stocks and bonds, tax-free and taxable income, options and commodity trading, annuities and life insurance, tax shelters, retirement plans, bank accounts and checking plans, and mutual funds and money market mutual funds.

Brokers offer some of the best money market funds with a wide choice of where to save your money. Dean Witter/Sears' Liquid Asset Fund, with its objectives of high current income and preservation of capital and liquidity, has become one of the largest money market funds available today. If you want even more safety, they have a U.S. Government Money Market Trust which is wholly composed of securities that are issued or guaranteed by the U.S. government or its agencies. The idea here is to give you high current income with the confidence of government securities. If taxes are a problem, you can save in a Tax-Free Daily Income Fund. The income is free of federal income taxes, but usually not state income taxes. Ask a broker for a free prospectus if you're interested in learning more about these money funds.

In an attempt to tie all of their products and services to gether, Merrill Lynch began offering a Cash Management Account (CMA) in 1978. The account, in all its variations, has become the brokers' main weapon in their war with the banks and thrifts for the consumers' dollar. Merrill Lynch's four-year monopoly allowed it to establish its service as the generic form in the public's mind. I'm reminded of the current television commercial of a three-masted sailing ship sliding across my screen telling me that if I hop on board I can have the captain manage my financial affairs. This is not a Cash Management Account, I'm informed, but a classier version, the Financial Management Account (FMA). E. F. Hutton tells us that "A securities account, no matter how you slice it, is no better than the broker who's behind it." They believe their Asset Management Account (AMA) "is an investment vehicle providing a combination of features no one else is offering." I have never quite grasped how brokers can have a different name for a CMA and yet all be offering the same thing.

Cash Management Accounts, with an entry fee of around $20,000 or more in cash and/or marketable securities and an annual fee of $100, are de rigueur for major financial institutions that feel they must offer some variation of the account. For status-seeking investors, having someone else manage their cash in a CMA ranks alongside carrying a Gucci purse or flashing a Rolex watch at a dinner party.

Cash Management Accounts under any name offer five basic services: a high-yielding money market fund into which your idle cash, dividends, or interest income is swept automatically by computer; check-writing benefits; a credit card or debt card for cash withdrawals; some form of Wall Street margin account; and, of course, brokerage services with the broker offering the account. With competition intensifying, many banks and thrifts are offering their version of CMA by sweeping idle money into money funds and providing discount brokerage service. The appeal of accounts that manage your assets is that they provide overall financial services while they turn your idle cash into working money.

Bonds

Now let's look at some new variations on an old theme, in which brokerage houses, noting banks' and thrifts' success in grabbing money with their new savings plans, are now developing customers, using their horde of salespeople. Stodgy bonds, once a surething investment for the heavy-wallet crowd, are now proving to be a hot way to attract the small saver back into the brokerage office.

Bonds fall into three major areas: regular bonds, tax-free bonds, and zero-coupon bonds. They are issued primarily by people who want the use of your money to make even more money. The federal government is the biggest issuer of bonds (and notes), and, to keep its financial house from collapsing, Uncle Sam goes to the money well with a big bucket. By being a voracious bully around the money well, the Treasury is responsible for the direction of the interest rates. That's because, by some estimates, the Treasury soaks up more than 75% of net private savings this year.

To give you some idea how big the government's appetite for money has grown, following the 1969-70 recession, deficits absorbed about 25% of net savings in the first two years; after the 1973-75 recession, the Treasury absorbed 49% of net private savings in the first year of recovery and 65% in the second.

Bonds are also issued by states, cities, corporations, banks, savings and loans, and anyone who feels that paying you a fixed interest rate and locking up your money is a very cheap way to run a government or operate a business.

Bonds are usually sold in $1,000 denominations, with the minimum sale five bonds, or $5,000. (Unit-investment trusts, which we'll cover later in this chapter, have lowered the minimum purchase to only $1,000.) Like stocks, most bonds can be traded on the exchanges around the country, but some can be repurchased only by the issuer. Bonds can pay interest (and part of the principle— like a home mortgage, in reverse) and some, like zero-coupon bonds, pay no interest at all. To give you an example of how brokers can package attractive investment opportunities, let's look at a new way to save involving bonds.

The Brokers Way to Save

In the crazy world of high finance, banks and thrifts are spending millions to convince us that an 8% return makes sense, even if we have to give back from one-third to one-half of the earned interest to Uncle Sam. Brokers, seeking a way to fight back against the popular money market account, hatched the Municipal Investment Trust Fund (MITF). Then, for the pile of cash—running into the billions—still not committed to common stocks and waiting for safer harbors, the brokers came up with Unit Investment Trusts (UITs) as a safe alternative to insured money market accounts. Small investors began to get the bug.

Unit investment trusts are easy to understand. They are a group of bonds, much like a mutual fund, put together in a trust and offered in units of $1,000. You can write checks on your trust, you have a choice of when you receive your interest, and you can choose to automatically reinvest your income to get the benefits of compounding. Sales charges are usually built into the UITs. The interest rate is your net return after expenses and sales charges.

It's important that you understand the difference between a bank or thrift money market account and a unit investment trust of bonds. A money market account is a fixed-asset account. If you invest $5,000 today, the value of your account will remain $5,000, plus earned interest. The insured money market accounts only let you know that if the financial institution goes broke, the government will step in and return your original investment. Your safety is a promise that your $5,000 initial investment won't be worth any more or any less than $5,000 in the future. Bonds, on the other hand, have a shifting value—like stocks, their value can go up or down. If interest rates rise, the value of your bond will fall, if interest rates fall, the value of your bond will rise.

If you buy bonds, any bonds, you need to be sure you have ready liquidity at the then-current market value. If interest rates rise, you may want to sell your bonds and cut your losses. That's the risk of buying bonds. It's a risk you can learn to master. It's also similar to the risk you already run when you lock up your savings for a longer term in a fixed-interest savings account.

In 1983, the smart money was rushing into unit investment trusts of FSLIC-protected municipal tax-free bonds. A loophole in the way Federal deposit insurance could be used was making a mockery of the carefully managed consumer saving plans advertised by the banks and thrifts. At a time when money market accounts were paying 8%, the new tax-exempt municipal bond trusts were paying about 9%. Big banks (yes, they were offering tax-free money at higher rates than their widely advertised money market accounts) and brokers were raking in the money.

In a 33% tax bracket (where most families with two incomes usually find themselves), a 9% tax-free bond actually earns you about 15% before taxes. An FSLIC-protected money-market account earning 8% only nets you about 5% after taxes.

1983 also saw the introduction of the Government Securities Income Fund, GNMA series, and Unit Investment Trust. The trusts stashed their money in *Ginnie Maes*. (Government National Mortgage Association—GNMA—backs mortgages for FHA/VA insured mortgages as a way to bring investment funds into the real estate market, where they are guaranteed by the full faith and credit of the United States.) Single-family, Ginnie-Mae-backed mortgages (the most widely-issued type) have a final maturity of either fifteen years or thirty years, but when they are locked up in a trust, with each unit sold to the public for $1,000, you have an investment with a high degree of liquidity. By locking up government-backed Ginnie Mae mortgage bonds, the brokers were able to offer initial interest rates of as high as 12.5%, net after commissions, with no charge to redeem or sell. The government securities income fund became a natural way to fight back against the banks and thrifts.

Ginnie Mae investment trusts can be an excellent way to save your money, often at interest rates much higher than insured money market funds, and with almost the same liquidity. While Ginnie Mae unit investment trusts continue to pay above-market interest rates, some investors will get their money back ahead of schedule and have to reinvest it at lower yields. That's because the actual yield on a group of Ginnie Mae bonds can drop when the higher-interest mortgages are refinanced, as interest rates fall.

Unit investment trusts claim, however, that because they offer diversification—their portfolios contain securities from a number of mortgage pools with a range of mortgage rates—their yields are less sensitive to swings in interest rates than short-term money market accounts.

You can buy newly issued Ginnie Maes directly from GNMA, but that takes a minimum of $25,000. If you don't want to shell out more than $10,000, you can invest in the secondary market through a broker. But the easiest and least expensive way to get started is to buy $1,000 units in the unit investment trusts.

Since Ginnie Maes are bonds, you'll need to remember that the payment you receive each month contains not only the interest earned, but some of your principal as well. Even when interest rates are steady, your monthly interest income can fluctuate, as the underlying mortgages that make up the unit investment trust are paid off.

You'll hear banks and thrifts warn you that if interest rates rise, you could lose money when you invest in bonds. That's true, but what they don't tell you is that with something as liquid as Ginnie Mae unit investment trusts, where the major brokers maintain an active market, you can cut your losses very quickly—something you might find difficult to do if you're locked into a long-term savings account.

Zero-Coupon Bonds

Zero-coupon bonds pay no interest, not a cent. A new idea, the brokers declared; the easy way to make your money grow.

78

Remember when patriotic Americans scrambled into U.S. Savings Bonds? Where for $18.75 and a ten-year wait, you could buy a $25 bond. Well, zero bonds put them to shame. The idea of zero-coupon bonds is that you buy them at a deep discount and collect the full face amount of the bond at maturity. The splashy ads tell you that with zero-coupon bonds you can earn a true compounded yield and lock in high rates of interest without the worry of reinvestment. To grab the small investor, minimum investments were lowered to as little as $250 or $300 per bond.

In what seemed at first blush too good to be true, brokers and banks offered to take $4,500 and in seventeen years hand you back $30,000. Give them $10,000 and they'd give you back a startling $250,000 in thirty years. In 1982 zero-coupon bonds made a big splash. Merrill Lynch ran full page ads about "A remarkable new investment opportunity," their new TIGRs (Treasury Investment Growth Receipts) with the added security of a U.S. Treasury obligation. Banks began selling zero-coupon bonds called Discounted Negotiable Certificates of Deposits. In the rush to buy zero-coupon bonds and lock up their money long-term, most investors forgot that the people who were so eager to take $5,000 now for the privilege of giving you back $30,000 later obviously felt they could do much better than that with the money you gave them. I believe they can too.

What's important to remember about zero-coupon bonds is that the earned interest—the difference between the purchase price and par—is treated by the IRS as ordinary income. In other words, you'll be taxed on the income you don't receive on zero-coupon bonds. This has forced *zeros* (as they are known among the more soporific brokerage crowd) into retirement plans and investment programs for low-income taxpayers, such as children. In IRAs, for example, the earned-interest income is tax deferred, avoiding the problem of taxing unreceived income.

Zeros can be used to help send a child to college. Suppose that in eighteen years you'll need $56,000 for your child's education. If you invest $6,500 in a zero and give it to your child, so interest income will accumulate with minimal tax liability, in eighteen years the child could start receiving about $14,000 a year for the next four years . . . with taxes already paid.

I do not recommend zero-coupon bonds except for certain unique situations where they may fill a need.

Tax Shelters

For well over a decade, high-bracket individuals have been persuaded to invest in what are euphemistically called *tax-favored investments* as a way to slash their personal income taxes. For those who were risking only fifty cents on the dollar, sometimes less, the ideas were crisp and convincing. In brief, here's how tax-sheltered investments work. A general partner forms a company, raises capital, and becomes responsible for the management of the new venture. Limited partners (investors) are then asked to put up money with the idea that, having once advanced their shekels, that would be the limit of their risk in the new venture. Since tax shelters are formed as partnerships, any profit or loss flows through to each individual limited partner in relation to his or her investment in the project.

For high-bracket individuals facing the intense heat of the IRS, the prospects were as inviting as the express lane on the tollway to Easy Street. The more the loss, the more attractive the investment became. Many tax shelters turned out to be just what they were intended to be: heavy tax write-offs in the early years, profits in the later years, followed by a sale of the assets with substantial capital gains. But tax shelters (often called limited partnerships, after the investors who put up the capital) can also be as varied as some of the larcenous characters who dream them up. If big losses attracted investors, they'd go off on a major spending spree. If early tax write-offs were the key, they'd make the deal irresistible, offering to deduct from current taxes the entire first year's investment. Always searching for ways to make your money work harder for you, the more adventuresome general partners began to dangle the prospect of deducting even more. Put up $10,000 and deduct $15,000 from taxes the first year.

Unfortunately, as more tax shelters became available, the competition forced many general partners, who offered the tax-saving deals, to raise the wind and blow dust into the face of the IRS. When the storm subsided, the IRS cracked down on the high-initial-tax deductions offered by some of the more venturesome limited-partnerships. The Tax Equity and Fiscal Responsibility Act of 1982 (TEFRA) cut back even further on the tax write-offs. The rate reduction effective in 1983 has made it more important than ever for investors to consider pretax economic merit before investing in tax-advantaged investments. These new depreciation-recapture rules are not favorable to most investors.

Other recent changes should be just as frightening. In addition to the interest you pay on back taxes, there is a new penalty of 10% on any underpayment of taxes over $5,000. And that is not deductible.

The simple fact is that the business of tax shelters has always been a risky one for investors. If tax shelters are risky and often simply a tax dodge, why are they so popular? Because the tax savings of well-managed tax shelters can be breathtaking—you can literally make money using the money that normally would have gone to Uncle Sam. In recent years, it's become fashionable during dinner party conversations to brag about heavy tax write-offs in cattle feeding, oil and gas drilling, catfish, chinchilla and mink breeding, almond growing. But this was only the beginning. When the government tossed out the carrot of sharply higher tax savings to encourage energy development, the tax shelter people were ready.

The desire to avoid paying taxes can cloud the minds of the most intelligent people. The newest craze became building giant windmills to generate electric power. The fact that wind sufficient to turn the enormous blades and generate electric power might occur only half the year did not deter the promoters. Far from taking the wind out of their sails, the tax shelter people built more windmills. Windmills, it turns out, were built principally to save taxes, not to catch the wind.

A recent windmill tax shelter offered federal investment tax credits, federal energy tax credits, and state energy tax credits. The $20 million offering was available in units of $5,000. In an age awash with great ideas, however, windmills may not be one of them.

Because of their highly speculative nature, tax shelters, or limited partnerships, are usually sold only to individuals with high incomes and substantial net worth. They are not liquid and cannot usually be sold once the tax shelter has begun. Their attraction is based on the assumption that the IRS or Congress will not change the tax rules until the project can be completed and sold—an assumption that is coming under increasing question as the nation's budget deficit continues to grow.

The latest tax shelter caper is not a tax shelter at all. Designed to catch middle-income investors, the new limited partnerships generate cash, rather than tax benefits. These partnerships are being structured to appeal to IRA and Keough plan investors by offering limited partnerships in real estate: they're being sold in $2,000 units (the maximum yearly investment for an individual that is tax deductible). With the limited partnerships' ability to pass through tax-deferred profits and capital gains to individual IRA and Keogh plans, sales will continue to surge, possibly topping a staggering $4 billion in 1983.

Stocks

If you've invested in common stocks, you need to maintain a clear picture of what they cost, their current value, and, most important, what their prospects are for making money. Your data sheet should fit on one piece of paper. Keep your back-up documents stashed away. Most experts say, and I agree, if you're an individual investor in stocks, prune your holdings to include no more than ten. Even then, if you can't afford to spend at least one evening a week seriously studying your investments and your moves in the market, you should consider mutual funds, or arrange for a professional to take over your portfolio. Full-time analysts, I'm told, with hundreds of millions of dollars to invest, have only fifty stocks to watch. Their list is slim enough to carry in their coat pocket.

Once a month, evaluate each stock as if you were considering its purchase. One reason small investors fail on Wall Street is that they ignore another eternal truth about the market: If you would not buy your stock with today's dollars, you should not own it with yesterday's dollars. The best strategy is often to sell the stock and not try to swim against the tide.

Often, you'll have to make the decision to sell on your own. Full-service brokers generally will avoid giving clear-cut "sell" signals, not only because too much downbeat advice is bad for business, but because in many cases the brokers' own research department may have recently had the stock on its internal "buy" list. In many cases, but certainly not all, a broker's "hold" recommendation (when the brokerage firm does not recommend purchase) is often your advance warning to unload your stock. If you think I am spending a great deal of time trying to get you to develop a sense of timing on the sell side, you are right. The problem is that most of us are not equipped to sell quickly. Our gambler mentality takes over.

If you're really committed to the stock (it's been in our family for some time; it's a friend) you might even consider taking advantage of its price weakness to buy more shares. Don't. Remember, if you wouldn't buy the stock if you did not already own it, don't buy it now. I don't believe in averaging down. Mutual funds have sold millions of shares of stock on this theory, but buying an individual stock simply because its price is falling is like being a gambler who sits in a casino and says I'll quit when I break even.

Stock Index Futures

Millions of investors, in fact, have found a better way to gamble on the market. Stock index future trading has caught on big. Stock index futures are a new money magnet that enable people to play the market without buying individual stocks. Investors simply stake cash on whether a particular market index will rise or fall. "It's a lot simpler than buying individual stocks," an avid player said. "I'm a crapshooter anyway, and I like the action in this fast market." The Federal Reserve Board believes its popularity stems from a market that combines the high stakes and fast action of commodities with the public appeal of the stock market. "For the speculator, this is a hell of a way to play the market," says Richard Plotkin, banking regulator for the Feds.*

Almost any index is fair game for writing future index contracts. The idea started in 1982 when the Kansas City Board of Trade started trading future contracts in the Value Line Stock Index; it quickly spread to the Standard & Poor's Index and the New York Stock Exchange's composite index. Trading volume doubled and redoubled—today it's reached about $3.5 billion—the equivalent of a ninety-million share day on the New York Stock Exchange. On twenty-eight consecutive trading days, when the game was growing in popularity, dollar volume in index futures exceeded that of the Big Board.

A future contract is simply a standardized, exchanged-traded contract to buy or sell a fixed amount of a specific asset, at a predetermined future date, for a currently determined price. Stock index futures are a little different from other futures, in that there is

---

*The Wall Street Journal, May 4, 1983, page 1.

no underlying physical asset. The arithmetic of stock index futures works like this: The value of a contract is set at $500 times the level of the index. If the index was, as in our example, 90.00, then one contract would be worth $45,000 (90.00 times $500). The initial margin (down payment required by the exchange to buy one contract) is set by each exchange; let's say, in our example, it's $3,500.

Then each 1.00 shift in the index moves the value of a contract up or down $500. You can close out your future contract at any time, and most do before they expire, and you take your gain or loss at that time. The stock index future game is relatively cheap to play, giving the public access to leverage it hasn't had since the late 1920s. With all the thrills of an investment video game, Americans are dabbling in index futures in record numbers. "What the hell," one devotee said, "it beats trying to figure out what stock to buy; you just bet on them all."

The IRS is faced with a problem: When is the stock market a gamble? Since stock profits are treated differently from gambling profits by the IRS, is gambling on the rise or fall of a market index the same as buying a blue chip stock? Of course not, but buying stock indexes on the future market rise or fall, rather than investing in the market itself, poses arcane, unpublicized issues that the IRS has only begun to address. Tax experts believe the gambling issue is one of interpreting the law. But then, all investing may be a gamble, and that's what makes it so interesting.

Henny Youngman may have had a better grasp of the stock market than the brokers who daily stride the creaky wooden floors of the New York Stock Exchange. Youngman is reported to have told of a compulsive gambler who bet on every basketball game his bookie could find. After a few weeks betting on fifty or more basketball games—and losing every bet—he called his bookie and asked, "How many basketball games today?" The bookie shot back, "No basketball games today, but there are two hockey games." "What do I know about hockey?" cried the compulsive gambler. Maybe we should ask ourselves that same question: What do we know about stocks and bonds? Experts are often of little help; they have missed the market swings, tarnished their credibility, and separated millions of investors from their cash.

As long as markets go down, they will come up. And when they do, the bull market fever that sweeps the market when the Dow Jones moves into higher ground will bring a renewed interest in the stock market. And with deregulation, there are some powerful stock promoters about. The entry of Prudential Insurance, Sears, Roebuck, American Express, and other mass-merchandising giants will extend Wall Street's sales pitch deeper into grass-roots America.

The entry of banks, thrifts, and mutual funds into discount brokerage will expand the market for equities, sweep in the "little guy."

Before you soar into uncharted territory, let's put the stock market in perspective. The market's report card, flashed around the world on television, radio, and newspapers each day, is the Dow Jones Industrial Average. If the Dow Jones Industrial Averages are an accurate gauge of the market's performance, and not everyone agrees that they are (although they're by far the most popular way to measure the rise and fall of the U.S. stock market), then the market has been deadly to investors since 1966, the first time the Dow Jones peaked a little over 1000. In a world with extraordinary technology instantly flashing down a band of moving lights the Dow-Jones Averages in Boston and Albuquerque, with know-how to take a picture of the dark side of the moon and provide a scope of medicine so sophisticated that life-saving surgery can be performed on a baby inside a mother's womb, shares of ownership in our country's real wealth—common stocks—are one of the few things that have regressed.

In 1966 dollars, a Dow Jones at 1000 today would actually be only about 370. Put another way, in current dollars adjusted for inflation, the Dow would have to be at least 2700 to be the equivalent of a 1966 Down Jones of 1000. The only reason the stock market looks so good today is because its losing battle with inflation has been concealed by the Dow Jones averages.

If stock prices rise in the next few years, it won't be because of signs in the charts, volume on the Exchange floor, or newsletter gurus. They will rise only if the federal budget deficit can be brought under control, if interest rates can be kept low enough to encourage businesses to expand, and if the economy can generate enough consumer confidence to send Americans on a spending spree.

How Will Brokers Change in the Eighties?

The big brokerage houses are out to snare you. They'll offer an inviting prospect: a dumbfounding array of financial advice, planning, and products. In short, they'll look more like banks, insurance companies, and mutual funds. You'll be able to buy stocks and bonds, save your money with insured CDs, borrow money, buy insurance and real estate, open your IRA, and have them look after your money with their managed cash accounts. You have only two questions: Is it safe? How much will it cost?

Before you put all your financial eggs in one basket, remember the 20-80 rule of financial economics, where 20% of the customers provide 80% of the business. There will be a mad scramble for five- and six-figure customers as the once-clear line between brokers and bankers continues to blur and as financial deregulation eases up on regulations that once kept them out of each other's backyard. It's a good idea to check if you have enough assets to profit from many of these new services—and the higher fees that will go with them.

Money supermarkets will continue to spread. What's truly remarkable about the changing way we save and invest is how cheap it can be to gather money by toll-free numbers, the mail, and small shops in supermarkets and department stores. Some brokers are already cutting their charges, making it easier to save your money at higher interest rates. Whatever happens, you will come out the real winner.

4

MUTUAL FUNDS AND INSURANCE: THE GROWING WAY TO SAVE

When I ran into them last month, my good friends Bill and Nancy were standing inside a shopping mall, looking in the big windows at the sale signs.

"You know," Bill said, "it's dangerous standing here. If you look long enough, you become convinced you absolutely need that sweater."

"Maybe you do," Nancy said. "You look tacky around the house."

"How're your investments?" I asked, trying to rescue Bill from that sale-priced sweater.

"Not too bad," he replied. "Have you noticed mutual funds lately? They're playing the old vegetable game again, now that the come-on yields have disappeared from banks and thrifts. Nancy seems to understand what's happening better than I do."

Vegetable game? "What's that?" I asked.

"That's easy," Nancy grinned. "The price of carrots is finally coming down. Got some the other day for twenty-nine cents a pound, and they weren't shriveled at all."

"Carrots?"

"That's right, mutual funds are using a carrot to pull back the money now that you can get a slightly better yield, with far fewer restrictions than in a money market account," Nancy said. "It's true—Bill and I feel a lot more relaxed since we've gone back into mutual funds."

"Look," Bill interrupted, "they let us do so many things in one place. You know they let us have unlimited checking and personalized checks. They automatically track our spending by category for tax and budgeting ease, offer discount brokerage service, and give us a Visa or Mastercard. They let us pay by phone, give us automatic bill paying, give us credit card security and direct deposit, and offer us easy transfer of our funds from our bank and between one mutual fund and another."

Bill is my economic indicator. When he feels he's overcome the confusion of the banks, thrifts, and mutual funds and is secure enough to think seriously about that sale-priced sweater in the window, you know consumers' savings and investments are headed for better times.

"Perhaps a new pair of slacks to go with that sweater, and you won't look so tacky," Nancy said, as they waved goodbye and headed for the racks of clothing inside.

Until recently, keeping savings in the bank was mainly for cautious souls who wanted the umbrella of federal insurance and those who were so confused they preferred to deal with humans in the flesh at the bank and thrift than with a scary mutual fund salesperson or some distance voice at the end of some money market fund's 800 number. But suddenly, mutual funds are thriving on the same wave of deregulation that has opened up the banks and thrifts, and they are appealing to even conservative savers. They are using carrots, in an era of threatened rising inflation, that are even more attractive then locking up your money safely at today's interest rate.

What Bill and Nancy were talking about was the Investment Company Institute's (the mutual fund trade group) advertising campaign to illustrate how the special restrictions in the banks' and thrifts' money market accounts take a big bite out of your expected yields. A lot of banks and thrifts have been dangling the high-interest carrot, the ICI says. But now that banks and thrifts have dropped their early come-on interest rates, the funds are almost even with them. In some cases, in fact, you can get a slightly better yield, with far fewer restrictions, in a money market fund.

Money market funds may look and smell like savings accounts, but investors actually are buying shares in a fund that buys short-term, income-paying investments and then pays out the earnings (less the cost of fund management) to shareholders in the form of dividends. With minimums of between $500 and $1,000 to open an account and current interest usually paid on any amount in the account, the ICI says money market funds are a lot better than banks' and thrifts' money market accounts, which have a $2,500 minimum. You can earn 5.25% on your money market balance when your account falls below the minimum for even one day. When that happens, the ICI explains, not only are you back to the old passbook rate, but you could be hit with a service fee of $7-$10 for allowing your balance to fall below the magic number of $2,500.

Just as there is no perfect place to live, so there is no perfect investment. But the one that often comes closest for most people is the mutual fund. These funds put together a wide variety of taxable and nontaxable, growth and no-growth, and high-flyer and sitting-on-the-sidelines securities. They then sell their own shares to the public. What you get, at relatively low cost, is professional management of your money by people who devote their full time to keeping up with the changes in the financial marketplace. Letting fund managers select your stocks instead of picking them yourself makes good sense for many investors.

The workings of mutual funds make them easy for most of us to use since, with a moderate stock market attention span, we can select the funds that are closest to our comfort zone. Suppose you want a fund that has consistently climbed more than the market averages in bullish times, while not falling too swiftly in down cycles. You can find one. Or suppose you want to try for spectacular capital gains, aggressive funds that buy into fast-moving stocks. You can find them. Or if you want steady, solid income, you can look at money funds or bond funds that pay both taxable and nontaxable income.

Whatever fund you select, be sure you know yourself, know the fund, and make certain the two of you fit together. In the world of mutual funds, just like the stock market, sometimes there are stars that flash in the night, rockets that blast off only to fall back to earth. The trick in the decade of the eighties will be to avoid funds that give way to the speculative excesses that so tarnished the image of the mutual funds a dozen years ago.

Forbes magazine, which annually publishes the records of the entire mutual fund industry, calls them "funds for all seasons." Perhaps. But to be successful in mutual funds, as with any investment, you'll have to learn the difference between spring and summer.

The mutual fund concept has been around for centuries. An investor with $10,000-$15,000 obviously can't afford too many different stocks. But a group of investors, a few thousand of our closest friends, can get together and buy many different issues, take advantage of diversification. That's the fundamental reason we buy mutual funds. It's a way to reduce our risk by putting money into a large number of stocks, instead of just betting on a handful.

The unit price of a mutual fund, like the per-share price of a stock, is called the "net asset value." It's calculated by taking the market value of the fund's investments and dividing by the number of fund shares outstanding and issued to the public. The net asset value price of most mutual funds is published regularly in major newspapers.

Among mutual funds there are differences to be aware of. Load funds charge sales commissions (up to 9%, with an average between 8% and 6%). No-load funds have no sales charges. The load funds pay brokers and their own salespeople to ease you into mutual funds. The no-loads sell theirs through the mail, in newspapers and magazines, and with their powerful toll-free 800 numbers. Mutual funds don't manage your money for free. Both load and no-load funds charge a management fee ranging between .5% and 1% of the fund's total assets annually.

Bill, who had moved back into mutual funds in a big way, must have found something he liked.

"What kind of funds did you buy?" I asked, knowing that a man who was about to purchase an expensive sweater must have found *something* to feel secure enough about to run up a tab at one of the classiest men's stores in town.

"Look," he said, "I'm a child of the Depression. That's why I'm more concerned about losing money than about how much I make. I went into some conservative stock fund that'll make me some steady money as inflation eats away at the dollar; you have to pick your own.

"I don't like load funds," he added. "They cost too much. You don't need a middleman, so why pay a commission to invest in mutual funds. If you pay a commission, you'll be reluctant to lose that money and sell when you should."

Bill was right, of course. With stocks or mutual funds, just as with individual common stocks, you've got to develop a sense of timing on the sell side, know when to unload your fund, and wait on the sidelines. The freedom to sell—and buy—is the key to successful investing. You can lose a lot of money in mutual stock funds if you adopt the old gambit of "buying, holding, and praying" that the stock fund you bought will go up.

If interest rates rise and the stock market slides, switch your money to a money fund. Then, if you catch the market on the rise, you can buy more shares than you sold and ride it back up.

There's no evidence that load funds perform any better than no-load funds, no matter what your broker may tell you. The problem is, with a load fund, the salespeople (sometimes called financial planners) are eating from your plate. Take a gander at what the meal can cost and how it can keep you from staying flexible in a changing market:

When you invest $1,000 in a load fund with 8% commission taken off the top, here's what your account looks like at the end of the first year:

At the start of the year	$920
Earnings at 8%	$74
Less taxes @ 33%	$24
Balance at year's end	$970

At the end of the second year, assuming the same growth rate and tax bracket, your average annual rate of return would be just over 1%—hardly a way to stay up with inflation! What you're doing, in effect, is buying a set of handcuffs when you pay out all that money up front.

When you search for a mutual fund, look into a larger family of funds operated by a single company. Each fund is designed for a different investment objective. Typically, you'll find a maximum capital gains fund, a money market fund, a fund for long-term growth, and an income fund providing either taxable or nontaxable income. When market conditions or your objectives change, you'll be able to move your funds around within the family of funds. Before you invest, look into the fund's attitude toward fund switching. Most funds have fairly liberal switching privileges: Some charge a nominal $5 fee, others limit your switches to, say, four or five a year. Find out whether you can use a toll-free 800 number. It can save time and make it easy for you to direct your investments as conditions change.

Mutual funds come in all varieties, but they usually fall into the following groups:

MAXIMUM CAPITAL GAINS. Funds that invest in stocks of small, fast-growing companies that offer near-term capital appreciation.

LONG-TERM GROWTH. Funds that buy stocks in companies with solid earnings, where fund managers believe there is a better than average chance for growth.

GROWTH AND INCOME. Funds that invest in blue-chip stocks for capital gains and income (dividends).

BONDS. Funds that invest in corporate bonds and preferred stock for taxable income.

INCOME. Funds that invest in stocks for their dividends and bonds for their interest. Income funds can offer either taxable or tax-free income. If you invest in a mutual fund solely for income, check carefully where the fund has invested its money. In its drive to show high interest rates, the fund may have invested in corporate CDs and bonds that may not pan out. Several funds invest only in government or government-backed bonds. They pay slightly less interest, but they offer you a high degree of security on your money. If you want tax-free income, several mutual funds invest in high-grade portfolios of municipal bonds. In many zero-tax funds, the interest is also exempt from state income taxes. As we've already stated, these tax-free income funds can be protected by FSLIC-insured CDs. Many tax-free income funds work on the same principle as money market funds—there's no sales charge, no penalties on redemption, low initial investment, and free telephone transfer.

MONEY MARKET. Funds that invest in very short-term debt issues for current income and easy access to your money. These are the funds that compete with bank and thrift money market accounts.
Like the stock market, mutual funds in stocks and bonds work best when you stay on top of the market. The idea, of course, is to invest in the fund when it starts to turn hot and move out for a

better performer when it's not. You'll usually do better by relying on your homework than by sticking with one fund through all the market's ups and downs. That's why it's better to check out the switching privileges before you invest, and why it's better to stay in no-load funds. They give you the opportunity to increase your investment when a fund is hot, without giving up 8% of your money going in. My list would include Value Line, Vanguard, Scudder, and T. Rowe Price.

When you decide to invest in mutual funds, you'll come face-to-face with a document that spills out clumsy jargon and looks so intimidating that you might at first believe you're being sued for your run-in with a shopping cart at the supermarket last month, instead of being solicited for an investment. Called a prospectus," this document is the Securities and Exchange Commission's way of telling you what's inside the fund. Its objective is to tell you, in plain language and in a brief way, the essential material you need to know, as well as supplementary information included to meet the technical requirements. The nuts and bolts are: the purpose of the fund, its investment record, how to acquire and sell shares, how the adviser is paid, who runs the organization, information on special programs like retirement plans, and whatever else the government considers "material." Generally, the latter is described as whatever "language lawyers have thrown in over the years to protect themselves."

The performance of the fund and it's ability to boost the net asset value of its shares and make you money will likely remain buried in financial tables. For good reason. When mutual funds strike out, they want another chance at bat. As one mutual fund manager said, "Who wants to see the box score for the last inning in bold face type going in?"

The SEC and the mutual fund industry would like to streamline the whole business of issuing prospectuses, let you discover in plain English how successfully a fund has put money to work, and what it can do for you. It's part of the financial deregulation that's sweeping in the financial supermarkets, where mutual funds will be for sale in simple transactions over the counter and by direct mail marketing.

After you've been tortured through a prospectus and you make an investment in a mutual fund, what you're really after is performance. The bottom line is: Can the mutual fund management take your money and boost your profits or income without spoiling your appetite for stocks and bonds? The secret lies with the fund or portfolio manager, who tends, on average, to be a lone wolf who seeks individual competition and the chance to match wits with the market. Some managers operate more aggressively than others, but they all tend to buy and sell their stocks and bonds at will. This individual responsibility generates a high-pressure, results-oriented drive for earnings and profits in a world where hundreds of mutual funds are striving to be number one. For the fund manager, compensation is tied to performance. If his or her fund does well, the payoff can be very large indeed; the incentives are very strong. Some fund portfolio managers make $350,000 a year or more, and they may be worth it if, unlike you and me, they can outguess the ups and downs of the market.

Mutual funds have evolved over the years into literally hundreds of special funds . . . like those for IRAs and Keogh plans that ignore income tax considerations; those for tax free income made up of municipal bonds; and those high-risk funds that invest in start-up, high-tech companies.

But if you're puzzled by what stock to buy in the current high-flying market, the mutual fund industry has designed a fund for you. Called the Equity Income Fund S&P 500 Index, the fund's portfolio includes stocks used in Standard & Poor's stock index of 500 issues. Unlike the usual mutual fund, the stocks in the portfolio aren't managed. Fund managers simply use the money from new purchasers to buy as many stocks in the index each day as the new money permits. The percentage of new money going to each stock is based on the current weight of each stock in the S&P 500 Index. For example, since IBM makes up 5.87% of the index, that amount of money would go to IBM stock; and 0.01% would go into Pabst Brewing Company stock.

The fund, with a $1,000 minimum, pays a monthly cash dividend. More sophisticated investors could hedge their positions by buying or selling the S&P 500 Futures Index traded on the Chicago Mercantile Exchange. The idea, one mutual fund manager told me, was to "create, to the extent feasible, a portfolio that will substantially duplicate the S&P 500. That way," he went on, "you can own the entire stock market—or at least the major portion of it represented by the S&P 500."

The chance to buy 500 stocks at once will appeal to many

individuals who would like to "play" the market rather than let a broker search for ways to make their money work harder. The Equity Income Fund S&P 500 will dangle some irresistible bait: the chance to let your investment grow as fast as the stock market itself. In 1982, the S&P 500 Index rose 14.76%.

If you find even the most aggressive mutual funds too tame, you can play the game another way. You can buy the stock of the investment companies that run the equity funds. Since assets in common stock funds have soared to about $60 billion, close to double their totals a year ago, the investment companies have done very well, too. Their stock rose to almost double its price from the middle of 1982 to the middle of 1983. How each company fares will depend on the impact of its advertising and how it meets the increased competition in the deregulated marketplace. In the past, if $250 was drawn to the investment company for every dollar of advertising, the fund could do quite well. Before deregulation and the advent of the bank and thrift money market accounts, some investment companies were garnering as much as $500 for each ad dollar.

What does the future look like for mutual funds? Like banks and thrifts, some mutual funds are going to be squeezed out of the market, unable to attract the investor and saver as deregulation heats up and the bigs take over more and more of the financial markets.

Deregulation of sales charges will come as it has for the discount brokers. With it, the Securities and Exchange Commission will give mutual funds greater freedom to negotiate with customers what sales commissions they should charge. The SEC will allow mutual funds to establish any kind of fee schedule they want, up to a maximum of 8.5% of the purchase price. Once this rule becomes effective, many small mutual fund companies may find that the reduced loads (commissions) may make it difficult to entice brokers to sell their shares. And since brokers and financial planners have sold about 80% of the mutual fund shares (not including money market funds, which don't charge sales commissions), the reduced loads could hurt many of the largest funds as well. The remaining 20% of shares were no-load funds, sold directly by the funds themselves.

The SEC move is classic economic deregulation, last tried in 1975, when the SEC relaxed stock commissions. On the same basis, increased competition will cause the loads to go down, drive many brokers out of the mutual fund business, and increase competition from no-load funds.

I have never quite grasped the idea of paying as much as one year's earnings for the right to buy something that is readily available without charge. My friends Bill and Nancy understand this basic investment strategy and why you can't give away a fat sales commission before you invest.

"The man in the mutual fund commercial believes in giving away $8.50 or $9.00 out of every $100 that he invests," Bill said, "and that's because he must be one of those unique individuals who has enough money to stroll through life without worrying about how fast his investment grows."

"Exactly my opinion," Nancy agreed. "We got a best-selling book by one of the big names in financial planning who told us not to worry about the sales charge. What we were getting for all that money was the road map that leads us to the best-performing funds."

"You ought to have seen Nancy steam when she read that her favorite magazine's mutual fund survey listed the top performer as a no-load fund!" Bill said.

"You don't like other people eating from your plate?" I asked.

"Not if I can do as well as they can," he replied, "and I think I can."

Insured safety will spread to money funds. Stung by the success of banks and thrifts in attracting deposits with federally insured money market accounts, many of the larger mutual funds have bought banks in order to offer federally-insured money market funds. In an unprecedented step, the government gave Dreyfus Fund permission to set up a new national bank. This approval by the comptroller of the currency, fought over by the banks and S&Ls and the Federal Reserve Board—who are screaming bloody murder—further blurs the distinction between what mutual funds and banks can offer. Dreyfus opened the bank in 1983 in New Jersey, giving it the catchy name of The Dreyfus Consumer Bank. No longer willing to remain just a mutual fund, Dreyfus's bank will offer home mortgages and refinancing, personal credit, and new car financing. Fidelity, the big mutual fund in Boston, has purchased a bank in Salem, New Hampshire.

The Travelers Insurance Company has applied to the FDIC for

insurance coverage for its trust company subsidiary, Massachusetts Companies. In its rush to offer accounts with insurance protection, the big insurance company plans to have its trust subsidiary offer a money market account, much like that offered by banks and thrifts, that would qualify for insurance coverage from the FDIC. To keep from running afoul of the Federal Bank Holding Company Act, which bars banks from owning an insurance company or insurance companies from owning a bank, the trust company subsidiary would take deposits for money market accounts but not make commercial loans.

Yet another idea is to insure money market funds to guarantee that your net asset value won't fall below $1 a share. Since savers pay $1 a share to enter money market funds, the funds would provide insurance up to that amount. The Vanguard Group has worked out a deal with St. Paul Insurance Company. Minimum investment would be only $1,000—not the $2,500 now required by bank-and-thrift-insured money market accounts. Keystone Custodian Funds would like to be insured by The Travelers Insurance Company.

No one knows if there's enough insurance to go around, or if the mutual funds will offer both insured and uninsured money funds, but clearly there's going to be a scramble for saving dollars. A look into the future tells us that all savings accounts and money market mutual funds will come with some form of insurance and pay competitive rates. It's going to be costly for banks, thrifts, and money funds to hold onto their savers. The race for customers will spawn a new generation of fancy saving plans.

Life Insurance

To stay ahead in the money game, you need to know how deregulation has changed the life insurance industry.

Drastic new product changes and plummeting premiums have suddenly hit the life insurance industry. Consider this: two years ago, for a basic, term life insurance policy, a male, age fifty-seven, paid an annual premium of $1,274 for $100,000 of protection. Today, at the same age, a smoker pays about $665 and a nonsmoker only about $375 for the year's protection.

The reasons behind the falling premiums: people are living longer and paying premiums longer, and higher interest rates are lowering insurance companies' costs. What you aren't being told is that reinsurers (companies to which your life insurance company sells part of the risk on each policy) have been hungry for business and have cut their reinsurance rates drastically. The life insurance rate card your agent flashes in front of your eyes now has three separate rates. One is for healthy nonsmokers who have not smoked a cigarette for the past year. These lucky people, the tobacco institute's claim of prolonged good health with smoking not withstanding, can expect premiums about 60 to 70% lower than those of a few years ago. Another rate card is for smokers, who the life insurance industry now believes will most probably die of lung cancer. They can expect to pay about 30 to 40% less. And yet another rate is for those about whose health the life insurance industry is plainly worried. They are tagged with the name of "Sub Standard" and pay higher premiums depending on how long the insurance company believes they can continue to pay the premiums.

Another major factor in the sharp drop of premiums is the taxation of life insurance companies. Under loopholes in the tax laws, life insurance companies have been able to reserve—and thus avoid paying taxes on—amounts that equal four or five times the first-year premiums they actually collect for annual renewable term life insurance. These tax deductions for the first-year reserves for life insurance policies could change beginning in 1984. Congress is also looking for a way to tax the increasingly investment-oriented products sold as part of a life insurance policy (the cash value build-up for which taxes on profits are currently delayed until the money is withdrawn).

Deregulation allowing financial institutions to pay more for the saver's dollar has hit cash-value life insurance like a sledge hammer. For over a century, the classic, whole life insurance policy has been a major part of any sound financial program. Its appeal was based on three solid assumptions:

It forced individuals to save for family emergencies and retirement money that would otherwise be carelessly spent on pleasure.

It paid a modest return on invested cash when banks and thrifts were paying 3-5% and inflation was almost nonexistent.

It provided long-term death protection, usually with a level premium that would not increase as we grew older.

For the insurance company, whole life insurance was an ideal way to pre-pay future death claims. Unlike selling fire insurance to a man with a lighted torch in his hand, the whole life business had a built-in success formula. The insurance company simply collected the premiums (with the insured pre-paying part of the death claims with the savings element in the policy), paid its agents fantastic commissions (sometimes up to 60-70% of the first year's premium); and, for the last fifty years, often resembled a Klondike gold-mine.

But suddenly, in 1982, the life insurance industry began to unravel. The basic assumptions that had supported whole life (and much of the rest of the life insurance industry as well) crumbled in the face of radically changing economic conditions. For example:

• Opportunities to save money for emergencies and retirement expanded. Banks and thrifts began fighting for your savings, with high-interest, government-insured accounts. Congress made available IRAs and Keogh plans, and the insurance industry itself began pushing tax-deferred annuities. For individuals who were looking for smart ways to accumulate cash, tax-free bonds and IRAs were turning out to be a far better way to accumulate cash than investing in cash-value, whole life insurance.

• Major health improvements have skyrocketed the average American's life expectancy, and sharply higher interest income has slashed the rates for all life insurance, widening the gap between the cost of term and whole life.

During the last few years, the industry has counterattacked, introducing new concepts such as "re-entry term," "deposit term," "modified life," "adjustable life," "viable life," and "universal life." Here's what your agent means when he or she says:

TERM INSURANCE: Term insurance provides death protection only—you merely rent the protection for each year's premium. Each year the cost of your policy increases. The annual premium for $100,000 nonsmoker annual renewable term for a 30-year-old male is only about $150. Since young parents with families are most likely to need a lot of life insurance, term is often the best choice.

In spite of all the soothing advice you receive from the whole life salesperson about long-term protection and level premiums until you push up daisies, one fact remains: If you need death protection during your younger or middle years, it's better to spend $300 a year for about $200,000 of term than $300 for about $25,000 of whole life. As you pass retirement age, term insurance becomes very expensive, at least in today's dollars, and by then most people aren't likely to need much—or any—life insurance.

The old story about term insurance becoming too expensive to keep after you retire because its premiums increase each year as you grow older, while whole life with its level premiums for the life of the policy does not, continues to be told. If you buy term, the insurance agent points out, you could be forced to do without life insurance in retirement because you couldn't afford the premiums in your old age.

To persuade you to lock up your savings in whole life, "That's the money you'll need when you retire," the agent emphasizes. "Those cash-values will come in handy when you no longer bring home that paycheck." What you're not being told is that to use the cash-values for retirement income will usually result in the cancellation of the life insurance policy anyway. In either case, you end up without life insurance in your older years.

To us battle-weary consumers, veterans of more recessions than we want to remember, the insurance company's guarantee of a monthly check for the rest of our lives when we retire looks appealing. So we turn in our policy and take annuity. The message derived from all of this? Term or whole life, most Americans have very little, if any, life insurance in force after they retire.

The new term policies:

Re-entry Term is a new name for a type insurance that passes on lower rates to the physically sound insured who can pass a medical exam at specified intervals. If your health remains good, your rates can be kept under control. If you can't pass the medical requirements, premiums can skyrocket in later years.

Deposit Term is a new kind of term insurance that requires a large deposit when the policy becomes effective. The insured earns interest on the deposit during the "holding period" until the principal sum and accumulated interest are returned at the end of the deposit term, usually ten years from the date of the policy. The idea is that with a substantial deposit locked into the policy, you are unlikely to switch insurance contracts, even for a better deal, and thus you will keep the insurance in force.

WHOLE LIFE: Whole life combines protection with a forced savings feature. In the early years only a small part of your premium is used to pay for the "pure" death protection, most of the money is saved to cover the risk of death in later years. The savings part of the policy, called its "cash value," gives whole life its unique features of level premiums throughout your lifetime and a wad of cash to use when you retire. Most whole-life policies have a cash value that builds up slowly in the early years. (Often in the first and sometimes in the second year of the policy the cash value is zero to allow for sales costs.) Then it begins to build somewhat more rapidly until—around age 100—the cash value has completely pre-paid the death claim and equals the face amount of the policy. The cost of stockpiling this horde of cash is why the annual premium for a 30-year-old male for $100,000 of whole-life could cost about $1,200, while term could cost only about $150 $100,000 of protection.

The life insurance industry has not made it widely known, but the much-talked-about cash value of whole-life is really a pre-payment of the death benefit on the part of the policyholder. Let's say that your $100,000 whole life policy has a cash value of $25,000. The message delivered in the headline of the sale promotion material tells you that this $25,000 is yours. But is it really? You have no say over where the money is invested—or what interest you'll receive for locking up all this cash. The insurance company lumps your money in with millions of other policy-holders' and buys real estate, talks about yields of 15-17% on smart investing. If you borrow the cash value—at the current rate of 8% simple interest—you don't fool the insurance company staff. They didn't fall off the hay wagon yesterday. They'll simply deduct the amount of your loan from the death benefit. In our example, the $100,000 whole life policy will now only pay $75,000 in the event of your death—and you'll still pay the same premiums based on a $100,000 policy, plus the interest on your policy loan.

To catch the shifting preference of life insurance buyers, an array of new versions of the old, whole life policy has been dangled in front of the consumer. The main object of these new policies is to improve the traditionally skimpy returns of whole life policies. To avoid losing the big dollar customers to initially less-expensive term insurance, carriers moved aggressively into more glamorous offerings.

Modified Term Life increases the amount of life insurance in younger years. Modified term has a gradually increasing premium for a set number of years—such as three, five or ten years—and then converts to a higher-premium whole life policy.

Adjustable Life lets the policyholder switch between term and whole life. It gives you one contract to adjust your coverage and premiums as your needs change.

Variable Life offers a fixed premium and an investment-selection option, but it puts the investment risk on the policyholder.

Universal Life features flexible premiums with tax-free cash buildup. As of now, universal life is running away with the honors. More than one hundred companies offer the product, first introduced in 1979 by E. F. Hutton Life Insurance Company. The money you put into a universal life policy—called a "contribution," since, within limits, it is voluntary, goes into a fund from which the insurance company takes two payments each year. The first is a charge for the death protection, which, in effect, is plain old term insurance. The second is for company expenses, sales commissions, and profits. What's left over earns interest at a rate set by the company, or according to some agreed-upon financial index. The money in the account—the cash value—grows at a variable rate, not at a predetermined rate as under whole life policies. The attraction of universal life is based on the expectation that the policyholders' cash-values will be invested in high-yield savings accounts. However, as interest rates have fallen and the uncertainties about the tax-deferred gain on income inside the universal life policies increases, the policy has come under some question.

In fact, today, the old may be becoming the new. In some cases, the newer whole life policies can provide both life insurance and death protection and outperform universal life in the race to obtain life insurance/investment returns.

When I go into my favorite ice-cream store, I always buy a cone with two different kinds of ice cream. I like to get as much going for me as I can when I spend more than a dollar for two scoops of ice cream. Simply analyzed, universal life is like a two-scoop ice cream cone. One scoop is term insurance and the other an investment fund. Whenever you buy a package, the question is whether you can get a better deal if you buy the components separately. If you shop for the best term insurance policy and shop for the best place to save or invest your money, you can probably do better than if an insurance company does it all for you.

Insurance companies are finding out that the introduction of new policies is creating chaos with their older whole life policies. To deter their enormous book of whole life policyholders from switching to new universal life, or some other lower-cost term policy, many companies are conducting vast mailing campaigns, offering to increase insurance amounts and, in some cases, reduce premiums, to keep the older, more profitable policies on the books.

For older term policies, it's a different story. Just look at the policies, written before the life insurance rates took a tumble, and you can see why. These term contracts give insurance companies a chance to follow the contract—and the premium rates—that were in force when you bought the policy. It's a way to keep right on charging premium rates that no longer exist. It's an appeal to greed, and it wins.

Here's how it works. Let's say you have a five-year-old term policy, and you receive a renewal notice. Let's say I am your same age, and I want to buy that same insurance policy from your insurance company. My agent fingers the company's freshly printed rate cards with today's lower costs and comes up with my premium. You are a step behind. Unknown to you, the insurance company may be using the renewal rates in your policy that were in effect five years ago when you bought the policy.

Because life insurance rates have fallen as much as 50% for nonsmokers over the last five years, you could be paying almost twice as much for the same coverage.

Another problem life insurance companies face is a raid on their pocketbook when older policyholders borrow out their low-interest cash-values. And with high inflation and soaring interest rates, the tendency among American consumers to borrow on their life insurance is becoming harder to resist. What many people are finding out is that they can borrow against the cash-value of their old policies, which contain simple interest rates as low as 5-6%. (Policies issued today contain interest rates of 8%, or more, when the cash-value is borrowed out.)

This opportunity to spur deposits has not gone unnoticed by banks and thrifts. Many now offer a reinvestment plan called "Idle Assets." Policyholders can borrow against their life insurance and reinvest the loan in Idle Assets certificates of deposit. The banks and thrifts like it, it's a great way to lock up long-term money. Many policyholders like it because they can make extra income without risk or the trouble it would take to do it on their own.

Here's how it works. Suppose you have a 5% cash-value loan for $10,000. The tax deductible interest you'd pay the insurance company is $500. (To have the interest payments qualify as tax deductible, you must have paid any four of the first seven annual premiums yourself, in cash.) If you can earn $1,100 on a long-term deposit, you can show a profit of 6% on your Idle Assets. If you invest that money each year (the profit of $600) in an IRA, avoiding income tax for only fifteen years, you could have over $23,000 at your retirement; in twenty years, $43,000 . . . money you would not otherwise have.

Borrowing on a life policy reduces its death benefit by the amount of the loan. Thus, part of the insurance has already been paid in advance when you borrow the cash-values and it will not be paid again as a death benefit. Marketing schemes allow coverage equal to the loan under a group plan for those who want to maintain the full face-value of their current policy and still borrow out the cash.

The biggest news in the life insurance industry is the introduction of the "guaranteed replaceable policy." To make life insurance fit the mold of the new financial supermarket, the policy has to be sold like car insurance. You've seen the ads on television: "Bring in your old policies and we'll show you how we can beat the rates and save you money in the bargain." The idea behind the guaranteed replaceable policy is that the new insurance company, which will give you a new policy in exchange for your old one (at the same amount of insurance protection), is accepting the same risk of death as your previous carrier. In other words, if you have a $100,000 policy with ABC Life, and you can find a better deal, you could exchange it for a $100,000 XYZ LIfe policy.

The market has been tested and the going was so good that the financial supermarkets will soon jump into the race to grab your policy—and your future premium dollars—in a big way. Life insurance will join car and home insurance, all looking for the most competitive deal. Millions of middle-aged and older policy-holders, who avoided making changes in their old whole life insurance policies with the same zeal that a singer avoids laryngitis, will realize suddenly that the cash-values in their policies could be money in a bank or saving & loan. By switching to a term policy, they'll be told that they can get their hands on the money now.

Life insurance will undergo radical changes in the decade of the eighties. Buying life insurance and investing money will, for the most part, move in separate ways. If you have a life insurance policy and you are thinking about a change, be careful! Always find out whether you can qualify for the new policy before you surrender your old one.

Tax-Deferred Annuities

Because of a loophole in the tax law, tax-deferred annuities are issued by life insurance companies. Roughly a million individuals own annuity contracts, a sort of reverse insurance with which you pay the insurance company a large chunk of money up front (often paid over several years)—the average is $20,000—and the company agrees to dole out regular amounts over a period of years, or until you die. For example, $20,000 will buy a lifetime monthly income of about $175 for a male, age sixty-five, about $160 for a female, age 65.

The appeal of a tax-deferred annuity is that you can turn over to the insurer your savings and let them grow rapidly, because interest income accumulates tax-deferred until you draw out the money.

A tax-deferred annuity is a contract between you and the insurance company, purchased with one or more payments, with the deferred annuity payments to begin at a future date.

Within this framework, insurance companies began to market tax-deferred annuities like a bank savings account, a handy place to save your money and delay taxes. The plans were called "ever-bearing money trees." Since your original investment was made from after-tax income, the reasoning went, you could withdraw your principal tax free. The tax rules for insurance company annuities allow "isolated" withdrawals as simply a return of your original capital. The ever-bearing money tree made it possible to withdraw a part of your capital tax free each year, while the balance of the funds continued to earn high interest with tax-deferred income. In many cases, in spite of the withdrawals, the total assets grew each year, and in some cases, the fruit was ripening faster than the investor could pick the tax-free money off the tree.

Then Congress, with one eye on the Treasury's mad scramble to find money to keep the government afloat, took a chain saw to the ever-bearing money tree. The Tax Equity and Fiscal Responsibility Act of 1982 (TEFRA), for the first time in more than twenty years, overhauled federal taxation of life insurers and how they offer their tax-deferring plans. The new law set tougher standards for tax-deferred annuities, diminishing their appeal as short-term tax havens.

Now the investor can no longer take out money—up to the total amount of the investment—without paying taxes. Under TEFRA, the first withdrawal is assumed to come out of interest income, which is taxable upon receipt. Like an IRA, which has a tax penalty of 10% for early withdrawals, tax-deferred annuities now have a tax penalty of 5% when interest income is withdrawn from an annuity within ten years after purchase, or before the age of fifty-nine-and-a-half. Also, like an IRA, the tax penalty does not apply in the event of the death of the annuitant.

Now that the money tree has been closely pruned by the IRS, there is something else you should know. Front-end sales commissions have disappeared from the fine print. Unlike mutual funds, with the load charged against your account when your investment is made (front-end load), tax-deferred annuities have a surrender charge. The load can vary between 6-8% of the total amount withdrawn—principal and earned interest—during the first five-ten years. Some policies have a sliding scale, with the amount of the sales load declining over the years.

Because an annuity is likely to tie up a large chunk of your capital for a long time, you need to be sure you have all the facts before you invest. As we've already seen, your broker gets a big cut off your premium from the insurance company, and his or her recommendations may not always fit your longer-term investment objectives. Your funds are guaranteed by the insurer that writes the annuity. Many smaller insurance companies write annuities, and you need to investigate the company before you invest. If your broker or insurance agent states that you can't possibly lose your capital, don't bet on it. You can.

Sales of tax-deferred annuities have grown in recent years because of high, insurance-company-guaranteed returns and tax breaks, which made them attractive alternatives to municipal bonds or taxable money market funds. Today many investors are looking at tax-free mutual bond funds, IRAs, and Keogh plans as well as other tax-favored opportunities to overcome the basic problems with tax-deferred annuities: they are not liquid, they carry high, surrender sales charges during the first ten years, the original investment is not tax deductible, and the taxes on income are only delayed, not tax-free.

To catch the shifting investors' preferences, insurance companies have come out with a new variable annuity, offering four choices of investments. The idea is to increase performance by letting you make your own "market timing" decisions. Called a "wraparound," these multifund plans typically include a money fund, a stock fund, or a fixed-interest bond fund, with which you can split your money or move it around as market conditions change.

Tax-deferred annuities can be an excellent way to play your retirement. They pay high, guaranteed (by the insurance company) interest rates, offer complete management of your money, and, since they are an insurance policy, avoid probate.

But a word of caution: The tax status of tax-deferred annuities continues to rumble around the halls of Congress. Changes can yet occur that could further chip away at the tax advantages now offered by tax-deferred annuities.

How Will Life Insurance and Mutual Funds Change in the Eighties?

Life insurance companies and mutual funds are moving rapidly toward becoming part of the financial supermarket of the future. Their agents and salesmen are offering a wide variety of mutual funds, discount brokerage services, money market accounts, life, car, and home insurance, and, of course, financial planning. To survive, they'll change from one-product companies to financial service firms.

There will be some survivors, but many won't survive. Insurance agents and mutual fund salesmen are being replaced by direct mail, counters in shopping centers, and the big banks and brokers who lust after the "float" that goes with selling insurance. The truth is, it's anybody's guess what waits down the road of deregulation. But one thing is already clear: the days of individual salesmen may be over. Giant retailers, brokerages, or even insurance companies can sell their products cheaper by going directly to the customer.

Insurance companies and mutual funds are rapidly moving into financial service companies. Their agents offer a wide variety of mutual funds, discount brokerage services, and savings accounts, while some life insurance companies even offer car and home insurance.

If all of this sounds like a financial supermarket in a Sears or Penney's department store, you're getting a better grasp on where insurance companies and mutual funds are headed.

5

KEEP UNCLE SAM FROM YOUR POCKETBOOK: THE NEW TAX-DELAYING GAME

For about a month after the income tax deadline I think about money more than I do at any other time of the year. I think of all the ways I wasted it. I promise myself I'm going to try to cut down on some of the silly things I do with it.

The best piece of advice I ever had about money came from my accountant.

After work one afternoon I strolled into John's office. I was making small talk about the pictures on his wall. They're all of him—doing in the IRS, opening some new tax shelter.

"Why do you have so many pictures of yourself?" I asked.

"I like to look at the past," he replied. "I like to recall special moments when I saved my clients from paying taxes."

"I bet you have a mirror tucked in your desk, don't you?"

He smiled that accountant smile, as if he was already feeling superior to me, a dummy about taxes anyway. "I'm still not convinced you understand how important taxes are and how much money you let slide through your fingers each year," he told me. "There's a fortune wrapped up in your paycheck. If you want to save money you've got to delay taxes *before* you save, or you'll just piddle away your fortune."

I found my mind wandering. "To tell the truth," I said, "I'm probably never going to change. Half the fun of having a little money is wasting it."

"Come on, don't be lazy," he said. "There must be some reason why your not playing the tax-deferring game."

I had to admit that I didn't have a good answer. "I've been trying to figure out how much of my income I waste each year buying those silly gadgets by mail, not how much I waste in taxes," I confessed.

"Maybe if you understood how simple and easy it can be to save taxes," he said, "and how much money you can quickly pile up when you don't pay taxes, you'd get aroused to take action." Taking out paper and pencil, he leaned across the desk. "I'll give you an example of how important an IRA can become."

I strained to be optimistic. I knew I needed all the help I could get.

"To have any hope of saving enough money for retirement, you've got to save taxes on *both* the original investment and all the interest accumulated over the years. Let me give you one example of the dramatic effect income taxes can have on your entire saving program. Let's assume you can cut and scrape and set aside $2,000 in a tax-deductible individual retirement account. Let's compare that with $2,000 in a regular saving account. In both cases you are putting money into your piggy bank, but in only one case is the pig getting fat!

"Unless you can grasp the fundamental concept of saving money *without* first paying taxes, you are never going to save enough inflation-cheapened dollars to retire without a constant strain on your fear bone."

"A melancholy thought, indeed," I sighed, "but with all the advertising campaigns the savings institutions are throwing in my face, it's tough to know what to do."

"Look," he said, as he began to write the numbers on his green-lined accountant's pad, "here's what happens when you ignore the powerful impact saving taxes can mean."

Total value of capital and accumulated interest at the end of the year with a single $2,000 investment and 10% interest. Assume interest and the tax brackets remain constant during the saving period.

End of Year	IRA	Savings Account	
		33% Tax Bracket	*50%*
1	$2,200	$1,421	$1,050
2	2,420	1,516	1,103
3	2,662	1,617	1,158
4	2,928	1,725	1,216
5	3,221	1,840	1,277
6	3,543	1,962	1,341
7	3,897	2,092	1,408
10	5,185	2,537	1,630
15	8,350	3,500	2,081

He knew there was no point in getting overly complicated about long-term savings and I knew as soon as I looked at the table that I was a step behind the smart money. It was enough to keep me awake at night thinking about my hard-earned cash resting in a taxable saving account.

"Am I boring you?" my accountant asked.

"Well, if you must know, I feel a little guilty. I did pop into my favorite store and ran a little rampant the other day. Now you show me that without an IRA I won't have near the money I'll need later on. The worst of it is, of course, that over the past few years I couldn't have cared less whether I was in an IRA or not."

"I like to use this example," he said. "It always scares the hell out of people when they find out how much money they pay in taxes. Here's what the table really means:

"If you're in a 33% tax bracket, and most two-income couples are, you can save as much money at the end of the first year in a government-protected cookie jar as you can at the end of the next *seven* years with a fully taxable saving account! If you're in a 50% tax bracket, and that's no longer that hard to do, you'll save as much money at the end of one year in an IRA as you will at the end of *fifteen* years with a fully taxable saving account!

"Just multiply those numbers by ten and you can get some idea of the size of the tax bite over the next few years. The secret of saving money over any length of time is the magic of 'tax-deferred compound interest.' That's how big corporations do it with their pensions, that's how doctors do it in their gold-plated pension trusts. That's always been the secret of any retirement plan. I think you should understand the magic of compound interest," he said.

"Exactly my sentiments. How does it work?"

"If you save with a spousal IRA and you invest $2,250 each year, most of the money you'll have when you begin to draw it out won't even be yours."

"Who's will it be? I put the money in the IRA each year," I protested.

"That's the magic of tax-deferred compound interest working on your behalf. Look at this." He laid another chart on the desk. "The surging numbers tell the story."

The Effect of Tax-deferred Compound Interest on Long-Term Savings

Amount saved @ $2,250 for 25 years	$56,250
Compound interest @ 11% each year	$229,500
Amount at end of 25 years	$285,750

As savers we think we enjoy high interest rates now available on new saving accounts, money market funds and as investors the profits to be made in the stock market seem irresistible. What we've overlooked is that *it's not the money we save each year*, but tax-deferred compound interest that will ultimately provide the lion's share of our assets.

Part of the problem in understanding the importance of IRAs, or Keogh plans for the self-employed (which we'll cover later on), is that we're bewildered about how they work. It need not be heavy going to explore the world of IRAs and why they offer a head start on tomorrow, but sometimes we get carried away by the IRA frenzy. At the start of the new year when income tax time looms ahead, every time you pick up a paper or turn on the radio or television, you'll find a prospector picking his way through the financial underbrush seeking pure IRA gold. When it's time to sell IRAs, there's a lot of hoopla and not too much unbiased advice.

Don't let any financial institution con you into thinking it's doing you a favor by locking up your $2,000. Consumer savings will continue to be one of the hottest commodities in the financial world. Before you rush out and open an IRA, or if you already have one, find out what you'll need to know before you do battle with the

112

IRA sellers. You may be surprised at the options Congress built into the program, why IRAs will give you the biggest bang for your investment buck. In fact, IRAs should be your number one cookie jar for money.

Congress designed Individual Retirement Accounts in 1974 for pensionless people (those not covered by a retirement plan where they work) to tax shelter the lesser of $1,500 or 15% of their income each year. Congress made the deal even sweeter in 1982 when the *people's loophole* was widened to include all working Americans and the basic deductible amount was boosted to $2,000. Let's look at the ABCs of an IRA:

How much can I put into an IRA? Up to $2,000 per person (and under the new law this can be as much as 100% of your pay), $4,000 for a married couple with two incomes, and up to $2,250 for a couple where one spouse works. If you open an IRA with your employer, called a SEP-IRA, which we'll get into later, you can move into the fast lane for your head start on tomorrow: the maximum annual contribution is a whopping $15,000!

How can I open a spousal IRA? You can open a spousal IRA if you file a joint return and one spouse has no taxable earnings for the tax year. You can boost your contribution to $2,250, dividing up the amount between accounts in the spousal IRA in any ratio you choose as long as one individual does not receive more than the maximum amount of $2,000.

How often do I have to put money in an IRA? Each tax year you have the choice whether or not to make a contribution. You can contribute as little as $500 a year in some plans or as little as $50 a month in others. If a year goes by without a contribution, you can't make it up in later years.

When can I open an IRA? Any time during the year; in fact, the sooner you open one the longer your interest or profits can grow tax-delayed. The reason you find a media blitz in January or March is because if you open an IRA and make a contribution before you file your income tax return prior to 15 April, you can take a tax deduction for the previous tax year.

What can I put in an IRA? Cash.

Where can I invest my money? Almost any financial institution from banks and thrifts to credit unions, mutual funds, brokers, insurance companies and discount brokers. A nugget buried in the 1981 tax bill bans investments in collectibles, such as coins, stamps, antiques, or fine art. The money can't be used to buy life insurance. *How many IRAs can I have?* As many as you want or need, but, you're still limited to the same maximum contribution, regardless of the number of IRAs you open.

When can I take the money out? At any time. To keep your hands out of the IRA cookie jar, the Internal Revenue Service imposes a stiff penalty when you take the cash out early. On the money you withdraw before you reach age fifty-nine and a half, you'll not only have to pay the income tax you deferred when you put the cash into the IRA, but you'll also be hit with a stiff 10% tax penalty. To encourage long-term savings even more, the straight 10% tax penalty is *not* deductible. (The tax penalty does not apply in the event of death and in conditions of long-term disability.)

When do I have to start taking the money out? You must begin to withdraw from your IRA by the time you reach age seventy and a half. If you have not made withdrawals prior to that time you must begin a system of withdrawals that will, on a monthly or yearly basis, consume your assets during your remaining life expectancy.

Who will inherit my IRA assets if I die? You name the beneficiary when you open the account. The taxation of the money will differ depending on how the beneficiary receives the payment. If the IRA is paid out in a lump sum it will be included as part of the estate for tax purposes. If the IRA is paid out over a period of at least three years, it won't be taxed as part of the estate. If you become the beneficiary of an IRA, it's worth getting professional help. The tax questions can be important to you.

What if I make a mistake when I open my IRA? Under federal law, you can cancel an IRA within seven calendar days from the date your account is established. If you have opened your account with a bank or thrift, you'll receive the full amount you deposited in your account, less any interest paid, and you won't face any administrative expenses or interest penalty for early withdrawal.

In the lingo of finance, you also need to know the *can'ts*:
You can't use your IRA as collateral for a loan or try to get around the early withdrawal penalty by borrowing from your IRA.
You can't invest in collectibles, transfer real estate or other assets other than cash into your IRA.
You can't have your IRA attached by your creditors.
You can't put in more money than your maximum allowed contri-

bution each year. If you inadvertently exceed the maximum investment, you can take out the excess without penalty before you file your tax return, otherwise you'll be whacked with a nondeductible 6% federal excise tax on the excess each year it remains in your IRA. An easy way to correct an excess contribution is to reduce your next year's contribution by the amount of the excess.

You can't invest in an IRA with unearned income, such as money you receive from investments, stock dividends, rental income, pension payments, or retirement annuities. Contributions to your IRA must come from your paycheck as earned income.

In spite of the massive barrage of advertising, the slick three-hundred-page books begging you to learn all, that's about all you need to know about an IRA. But if you're a true money grubber like me, you're going to want to know the inside tricks of the trade that enable you to manage your money for a maximum payoff, not just shift your accounts around, sticking with what the banks and savings and loans are willing to pay. The eternal truths for saving tax-deferred income are good sense, diligent homework, and the chance to meet my accountant.

He gave me a guide for dealing with IRAs, the key points you need to know to take the mystery out of retirement accounts. They are crisp and convincing. The important points to remember are:

Types of IRAs

Basically, there are three: a Contributory IRA (the most common, the one where you make periodic tax-deferred contributions during your working life from your earned income), a Rollover IRA (where you "roll over" the assets you receive from a tax-qualified pension or profit-sharing plan where you work), and a Simplified Employee Plan (SEP/IRA—a retirement plan established by an employer using IRAs).

Let's take a closer look at two important IRAs that could make the difference whether you stay ahead in the money game.

ROLLOVER IRA. What's important to remember is that if you receive assets from your employer's retirement plan when you change jobs or when the employer's plan is terminated, you may put part or all of the money into a Rollover IRA. There is no limit to the amount of money you can roll over. By rolling over the money, you can continue to keep the assets and the future earnings tax-deferred until you take the money out. But the IRS's gift of continuing to delay the tax bite comes loaded with a steel spring trap: once you receive the money from your employer's plan you have only sixty days to put the assets into an IRA account.

If you have been making voluntary contributions into your employer's retirement plan, you'll also get this money back but you can't include it with the employer's money when you roll over the assets into an IRA. Your voluntary contributions, on which you have already paid taxes, come back to you tax-free.

The idea behind two different IRAs (Regular and Rollover) is to give you future flexibility in your tax-deferred planning. That's because if you make a regular contribution to a rollover IRA it can change its status, lose the rollover status of your funds, and you may not then roll them over into another employee benefit plan should the opportunity arise. If your Rollover IRA is maintained separately from your Contributory IRA, you should not make additional contributions from your paycheck to your rollover IRA.

For all our apparent daring and cleverness, this is not the place to make a mistake and try to back up. With reverse gear gone, I suggest you buy yourself some time—up to a year or more until you file your tax returns—to continue sizing up your options. Unless you desperately need a large chunk of the money, open a Rollover IRA and think about it. You won't lose anything by keeping the money you receive from your employer's retirement plan inside an IRA until you do your tax returns.

SEP/IRA. Called a Simplified Employee Pension, SEPs were designed to appeal to employers who believed full-scale pension systems were too expensive or too complicated. A product of the 1978 Tax Reform Act, SEP/IRAs must be established by your employer; you can't do it yourself. SEP/IRAs are nothing more than a group of individual IRAs, one for each employee covered under the plan. Once the employer's contributions are made into the SEP/IRAs, they immediately belong to the individual employee. No employee contributions are required. One big attraction to the boss is that once the SEP/IRA plan is established, the company is not required to contribute each year, as it would with a qualified pension plan.

Congress, in its eagerness to stem the gush of employer retirement plan terminations in the wake of the nightmare of paperwork imposed by the Employee Retirement Income Security Act (ERISA) in 1974, ended up giving business a blank check. The Wonders in Washington, for tax year 1983, will allow employers to contribute 15% of an employee's salary up to $15,000 into an IRA! You and I, if we work for a living, can contribute up to $2,000. We are a step behind. How in heaven's name can SEP/IRAs justify a tax-deferred contribution rate 750% greater than an IRA?

Starting with tax year 1984, Congress has come up with a cute gimmick to shame anyone with a mere $2,000 to invest in an IRA. They call it *sweetening the pot* and here's how it works. Employers can boost their contributions up to 25% of your income, or $30,000, and put the money directly into your individual SEP/IRA. But there's more to this *hide the money from the IRS* caper. Under the Economic Recovery Tax Act of 1981, if your employer stashes big dough away for you in a SEP/IRA, you're free to make additional voluntary IRA contributions up to 100% of your pay or $2,000, and if only one spouse is working outside the home, up to $2,250.

Here's how it works. Say you earn $20,000. Your employer can then contribute $3,000 to an IRA that qualifies as a SEP/IRA. As a smart money manager, you also make a $2,000 contribution to the SEP/IRA. At tax time, you must include the employer's contribution of $3,000 in gross income on your tax return, but you're entitled to a $5,000 deduction ($3,000 plus $2,000) from gross income for total SEP/IRA contributions. A neat way to rip off the IRS—if you can overcome one big handicap: you and your boss have to join hands to beat the tax man.

Sometimes it's difficult to bring this tax talk clearly into focus. It's not that we have trouble with the English language, it's just that the gimmicks Congress pushes us into sometimes fog over the end results. In fact, one idea like this—in which your employer puts up $3,000 and you put up another $2,000 out of your paycheck—could put you on easy street when you start opening mailbox checks. Suppose you're forty-five and you can make these contributions until you're sixty-five, at today's high IRA interest rates you could end up with an extra $360,000. If you're only 40, the results look better: $640,000. If you're 35, the results are spectacular: over $1,100,000! And most of that pile of cash, as we've already seen, will come from tax-deferred compound interest.

You may wonder why you didn't start your IRA earlier when you see how much money you can safely accumulate with tax-deferred compound interest. And you'd be right. In this example, every five years you wait, you cut the amount you'll have at retirement in half!

In the next chapter we'll tell you about other ways your boss can sweeten the pot without costing you a cent of taxes.

Changes and Transfers of IRAs

Another important point to remember is that your IRA need not be located at one financial institution forever. "Most people have a choice when they become concerned about their money and their IRAs," my accountant told me, "and one basic choice is deciding where to keep your IRA."

If you have your IRA money tucked away in a bank or savings and loan and new savings plans with higher interest spring onto the market, it's good to know that you can transfer your IRA from one financial institution to another as often as you like.

For now we are enjoying a respite from inflation. But times change, always have. Most of us believe stable prices are going to disappear, as they always have, to be replaced by higher prices for the necessities of life. Yet, we seldom think of our long-range financial plan and our IRA.

While you can transfer your money from one IRA plan to another as often as you like, there is a catch. In the lingo of the IRS, you need to know the difference between a transfer between IRA custodians and a simple rollover between IRAs.

Suppose you want to move your IRA from one financial institution to another. Decide where you want the investments to go and then approach the new money place and request that it get the money for you. It will send a letter from you to the trustee of your old plan and have the funds transferred. That's called a custodian-to-custodian transfer, in which you never get your hands on the cold cash.

If you take the funds out of one IRA and invest them in another (within the sixty day time limit) the IRS will call your action a rollover and limit you to one rollover a year on this money.

118

A change of investments within the IRA, such as a transfer among mutual funds within the financial institution holding your IRA, is not part of the IRA go-round. How you change investments within an IRA is your own business.

Admittedly this is heavy going. IRAs started out simple enough but after several major tax laws, designed to stem the hemorrhaging flow of taxes through the newly found loopholes, the program has become confusing to most Americans. Worse yet, it's become confusing to those who are trained by their financial institutions to help you open your IRA account. With high turnover and low pay, the "financial experts" in many money shops know little more than what they are told to protect the firm's business and what they read in the newspapers. To avoid wasting time chasing this *inside* information, you need to know that you can have two different kinds of IRA accounts. The kind you select will depend on your involvement and interest in your money during its growing period.

Additional IRA Accounts

REGULAR IRA. An IRA where the financial institution acts as your plan trustee without charge. Regular IRA plans are usually limited to banks, thrifts, and credit unions. You may already know this since banks and thrifts, lusting after IRAs as a source of relatively cheap, locked-in deposits, are spending huge sums of money to tell you their IRAs are free. What they don't tell you is that you are usually limited to their recommended, in-house, fixed-interest accounts with substantial early-withdrawal penalties.

If this is within your comfort zone, if you like the idea of using the same saving plans offered to all customers at the financial institution, and if you want a *hands-off* long-term saving plan, then a regular IRA is for you.

SELF-DIRECTED IRA. If you want to direct the investments in your IRA, you'll need to hire your own trustee. When Congress gave us IRAs in 1975, it required that the money be held by a trustee (someone who could tell the IRS when you reach into the cookie jar and take out the money). As we've already said, banks, thrifts, and credit unions usually provide this trustee service without cost.

In a self-directed account, where you retain your own trustee, you'll have to pay a set-up fee, usually between $25 and $50, and an annual administration fee, usually between $30 and $50. The fees are tax deductible, and they could turn out to be a good investment if you think you can keep your money rising at least as fast as inflation. With a self-directed IRA, you are free to pick the stock, mutual fund, bond, money fund, and even limited partnerships in which your account can invest.

You may wish to divide contributions among various investments and alter your strategies from year to year, depending on economic conditions. Like all investments, ask for complete information and read the fine print before you invest. Otherwise, you may discover your IRA has shrunk in value, and you won't be able to buy that retirement you hoped for.

A point to keep in mind when you direct your own investments in IRAs: In an IRA you need to forget about tax implications and examine the total return. Be wary of investments that are already tax-favored.

You want investments that will spring off high taxable earnings. If you're in your middle years you might want to look at some high-income investments, which are probably riskier but worth investing in because of their high returns.

Self-directed IRAs are available from brokers, mutual funds, insurance companies, and discount brokers. All these companies are actively pitching for your IRA money. Some offer lower set-up fees and annual administration fees, some even dangle the bait of free self-directed accounts. It's a buyer's market. Shop around for the best deal in your area.

Voluntary Contributions to Your Employer's Plan

Your employer may believe he has a way to make your money work harder for you, but be wary. When IRAs were expanded to cover people already under a retirement plan where they work, the law was also expanded to allow voluntary deductible contributions to your employer's qualified pension or profit-sharing plan. You can put into your employer's retirement plan and deduct up to $2,000 each year. The catch is that if you do, the amount of your contributions will count toward your annual IRA contribution limit.

In other words, you have a choice: you can tax deduct dollars going into your employer's retirement plan or you can tax deduct dollars going into your IRA, but not both.

If you want to stay ahead in the money game you should be aware of the fact that IRAs can be used for short-term tax shelters. Most people don't set up IRAs because they may want to tap the account before retirement or before they reach age fifty-nine and a half. As we've already learned, the way the IRS keeps our hands out of the IRA cookie jar is to impose a stiff penalty on withdrawals before we reach age fifty-nine-and-a-half.

But investors in average tax brackets and nearing age fifty-nine-and-a-half can put money into an IRA and take it out before retirement and still get the benefits of a tax shelter. Suppose it turns out you don't need your money for five years, you can play a winning hand with Uncle Sam. Let's say you're fifty-four with, say, five years to age fifty-nine and a half; then with an IRA you can put in $2,000 each year and cash out at the end of five years with a pretaxed total of about $13,500. In a one-third tax bracket, that's about $9,000 net. If you paid your taxes each year and earned the same return on your investment, you'd have only about $8,500.

Since withdrawals from IRAs are taxed on a calendar-year basis, if you withdraw in January you could *float* the taxes until the following April 15, beat the government at its own game.

Using IRAs for intermediate-term tax shelters requires a new decision each year based on when you anticipate cashing out. At some point, you may decide not to contribute any further and simply let the interest accrue.

The future for IRAs looks bright. Each year dozens of bills are introduced into Congress to expand the IRA program. Some seek to boost the maximum, up to as much as $5,000, and provide cost-of-living increases thereafter. Some want to allow either spouse to use either spouse's income to qualify for an IRA. In other words, if a woman stays at home and has no taxable income for the year, she could use her husband's income as if it were hers and qualify in her own name for the full benefits of an IRA.

But the best reason of all for starting to stash away your money in an IRA may be the expanded uses coming out of Congress in the next few years. I don't mean to indulge in make-believe, but I can honestly say that some of the most exciting uses for IRAs are still to come. For example, to encourage younger people to open IRAs, Congress is working on a bill to permit IRA funds to be used to help a person buy a house. The bill would allow pre-age fifty-nine-and-a-half withdrawal of IRA funds to purchase a principal residence without a premature distribution penalty, provided certain conditions are met. The money withdrawn must be used within ninety days as a down payment and the IRA depositor must live in the house as a principal residence for at least three years.

This is only one of many bills in Congress to allow IRAs to become joint-equity investors in our homes. The idea is that taxation of the money withdrawn from the IRA to help buy the home would be deferred until the home is no longer the principal residence or age fifty-nine-and-a-half, whichever comes first. Once the house is sold, the original IRA investment, plus the appreciation, could be returned to the IRA and continue to build tax-deferred until you draw out the money. The idea is quite simple: Along with other approved investments, your IRA money could also invest in your home . . . maybe even provide money to remodel your kitchen. The new IHA, or Individual Housing Account, is only the first of many proposed uses for IRAs.

In fact, IRAs are fast becoming the newest pork barrel in Congress. They have been such a bonanza for financial institutions that other special-interest groups are fighting for a piece of the pie. Mortgage companies now have a proposal in Congress to give homeowners a chance to pay off their mortgages faster than they have to. This new IRA would allow another $2,000 a year deduction ($4,000 for couples) for speeding up principal payments. The special-interest groups, trying to avoid the tag of budget busting, claim that the tax deduction for the homeowners IRA to speed up mortgage payments would actually lessen government red ink. The IRA tax deduction would be far less than the interest deductions over the length of the mortgage.

Like a return of the ill-fated All-Savers Certificates, the Reagan Administration is pushing yet another IRA that would permit $1,000 a year to be put into a saving account on which the interest would be tax-free, not just tax-deferred, for families earning up to $40,000 a year. The $1,000 could not be deducted from income taxes, like an IRA, but the amount could be increased when Congress seeks to boost savings. What now makes IRAs so attractive is that they can be made to scratch so many backs at the same time.

The going can become so good that IRAs might be all-things-to-all-people, a way to save for both before and after retirement.

Keogh Plans

Retirement plans for the self-employed work in a different way. Begun in 1962, and named after Congressman Eugene J. Keogh of

New York, who was mostly responsible for their passage, they are the government's answer to bargain-basement income taxes for nonincorporated business owners. Self-employed individuals (self-employed is defined by the IRS as being either a sole proprietor or a partner who owns more than 10% of the partnership) can open a Keogh plan only if they include any other employees with three or more years of full-time employment and who have attained the age of twenty-five.

Since Keogh plans were used as the guideline for the later legislation creating IRAs in 1974, most of the rules for Keogh plans are the same as those we've already learned for IRAs. Congress believes (or at least that's what we're told) that every working American deserves a chance to save tax-deferred money for retirement. Not necessarily an equal chance—that depends on the political muscle you can send up to Capitol Hill—but at least a chance. In 1982, when the annual contribution to IRAs was boosted $500 up to a maximum of $2,000, Keogh plans shot up from $7,500 to a whopping $15,000. In tax year 1983, you can tax deduct up to 15% of your self-employment income, up to a maximum of $15,000. But the small business lobby really struck pay dirt—preying on the cupidity of their congressmen—when they got the rules changed to allow Keogh plan participants to also have an IRA, lifting their total maximum contributions to $17,250.

Starting with tax year 1984, Congress will change the way Keogh plans work, move them more into the world of corporate retirement plans. Moving small business into the playground of the corporate pocketbook opens up a vast, and complicated, opportunity to shave taxes to the bone. Contributions can skyrocket up to as much as $30,000, with cost-of-living increases starting in 1986. And, remember, if you have a Keogh plan you can also have the full benefits of an IRA.

The opening date for Keogh Plans is different from that for IRAs. Unlike an IRA, where you can open an IRA in the following tax year and still take deductions for the prior year, Keogh plans must be opened (adopted and in existence) by the last day of the tax year—that is, by December 31 for persons operating on a calendar-year basis.

If you already have or are thinking about opening a Keogh plan, talk with your accountant or financial adviser before you make any further moves. The rule changes are so vast you'll need all the help you can get to take the maximum advantage of one of the greatest congressional tax giveaways ever passed.

Retirement Plans for the Heavy-Wallet Crowd

With Congress expanding the avenues for tax-deferred savings, those among us who really make the big bucks—doctors, lawyers, architects, dentists, and my friend the accountant—have carved out the greatest tax shelter of all.

Earning high income in the top tax brackets, they are managing to keep most of their money away from the IRS by forming professional corporations. If a dentist earning $150,000 a year decides that too much of his money is going to Uncle Sam, he puts a bright new shiny pension trust in his closely held corporation. He pays himself a good salary and dumps the rest of his income into his pension and lets the government pick up the tab.

When he gets a little short of hard cash, he borrows $10,000 or $15,000 from the pension trust, paying the going interest rate, which itself is tax deductible. And incidentally, the interest he pays on the loan is tax-free income to his pension trust.

Have you ever wondered, if you had really big bucks how much pension you could fund at your retirement? Currently, you'd have to struggle by on $7,500 a month, or a cool $90,000 a year for life. While the Tax Equity and Fiscal Responsibility Act of 1982 (don't you just love some of the names Congress comes up with to boost taxes) makes significant reductions in corporate retirement plans' funding, the tax savings for the heavy-wallet crowd can still be spectacular.

Tax-Sheltered Annuities

Your trip into the world of deferring taxes would not be complete without a glance at possibly one of the greatest pieces of preferential treatment ever accorded one segment of American workers. The Technical Amendments Law of 1958 allowed employees of privately supported, nonprofit educational, charitable, and religious institutions to exclude huge sums of their pay from federal income taxes. In 1961, the legislation was amended to expand the original pork-barrel section of the law to include educational institutions supported by public tax money. America's school teachers were the last group to step inside the tax-deferred elevator before the door was closed for good.

If you are one of the select few who can grasp the gold key—such as doctors at nonprofit hospitals, teachers, workers at research foundations, for example—the tax-saving opportunities can be breathtaking.

For starters, you can instruct your employer to contribute up to 16.6% of your pay into a Tax-Sheltered Annuity (TSA). If you earn $25,000, that's over $4,000 versus an IRA of only $2,000. In the second and succeeding years, you can reduce your salary up to 20%. What's more, with this Super IRA, you can also have an IRA and tax deduct another $2,000! The law also allows you to boost your TSA contributions using something called *past-service credits.* Unlike IRAs, TSAs allow a worker to go back and pick up years of employment with the nonprofit organization when no tax-sheltered contributions were made. This can be extremely attractive to older workers who, after their children are grown, have additional taxable income. The past-service allowance may be prorated over the future years of service if a larger level contribution is desired.

Let's look again at individuals with a $25,000 salary. In the first year, with a TSA and an IRA, they could tax deduct up to $6,165. In the second year, with a TSA and an IRA, up to $7,000 (or if one spouse does not work outside the home, up to $7,250). The maximum might be as much as $10,000 on a salary of $25,000—or 40% of income—by using both a TSA and an IRA.

Technically, you must instruct your employer to invest the money into a TSA on your behalf, but you are not required to report as current taxable income the money paid by the employer, subject to the limits in the law. You can ask your employer to pay this money into a TSA from either additions to your salary, a reduction in your salary, or a combination of the two.

What makes TSAs so handy is that, unlike IRAs, you can withdraw your voluntary contributions at any time without the 10% tax penalty that would normally apply to people under age fifty-nine and a half. You can, in effect, put the money in any time and take it out any time without a tax penalty. TSAs are excluded from the participant's gross estate if paid to a named beneficiary over at least two years (three years for an IRA). Like IRAs, TSAs are not attachable in case of bankruptcy.

If you leave your job with a nonprofit organization and lose your right to contribute to a TSA, you can roll over your TSA into your IRA on the same basis as a private retirement plan. I suggest that you roll over your TSA as soon as you can. You'll expand your investment opportunities and put the money where you can get your hands on it at any time.

Under the law, investments in TSAs must be made in annuities and/or mutual funds. Life insurance is also permitted with certain restrictions. You can invest in fixed or varable annuities or selected mutual funds, but your employer must approve the list of investments and actually make the payment to the insurance company or fund.

In the twenty-five years since the passage of the Technical Amendments Law, millions of working Americans have seen their tax savings, regardless of their age and income, all but disappear. Left with $2,000 each year, they often wish they had started earlier, that Congress had let them contribute into an IRA years ago, and now they are faced with no way to catch up. What they need is the opportunity to qualify for a TSA and make up for lost ground. A tax-deferral retirement plan that lets a $25,000 earner contribute as much as 28% of current salary in the second year with a TSA/IRA, while an employee of a profit-making company can only contribute 8% into an IRA, is pork barreling in the best tradition of Congress. If you have a chance to take advantage of a TSA where you work, open your Super IRA and let the IRS help you make your money grow!

6

FRINGE BENEFITS WHERE YOU WORK: THE NEW WAY TO BOOST YOUR INCOME

Our good friends, Bill and Nancy, were over for dinner last week.

"My company is offering a big deal in new fringes," Bill said, "something called a 'cafeteria plan.'"

"Sounds interesting," I said, deliberately making a wide-open question. "Tell me more."

"Here I am still trying to figure out rack-and-pinion steering and single-needle stitching in my shirts, and you come along and ask me to explain cafeteria fringes. In fact," he said, "if it doesn't grow, I don't know much about it."

"Some garden," Nancy teased, "three of his rocks died last week."

"I've noticed you've been a little uneasy," I said, "but if the company offered you a cafeteria plan you'd have a chance to run wild in the gift shop. You can save taxes by putting part of your income where you can get it, but Uncle Sam can't."

"Smashing," Bill said.

"While we're saving all that money," Nancy said, "you ought to see that plum jacket and white skirt—smashing is the word for it."

"What have you done with the cafeteria plan?" I asked.

"I'm still studying it," he sighed.

I figured what he really was saying was, "It sounds like a good deal, but I don't understand why."

"I don't blame you," I said. "Sometimes even I could cry when I think about what tax loopholes are doing to us. Last year Congress increased our taxes when we pay our own medical premiums, and now companies can use our money to pay the same bills tax free. That may not seem to make sense, but that's why cafeteria plans have become a first rate way to save money and taxes."

"Exactly my sentiments," Nancy said. "What can Bill do?"

"Traditionally, your company would offer you fringe benefits whether you need them or not. They come with the job. Now, however, what they're saying is that you have a choice about how to spend the company's fringe-benefit money. Like the case for Simplified Employee Pensions with IRA, SEP/IRA, when you and your employer can contribute up to $15,000 into an individual IRA, cafeteria plans let you spend money on a host of needs without first paying Uncle Sam."

"And if I don't need the benefits, I don't spend the money?" Bill asked.

"That's right," I said, "and if you do, you can use your money tax-free to get the job done. Cafeteria fringe-benefit plans work like this:

Cafeteria Plans

Cafeteria benefit plans let employees fill their plates with a choice of benefits and then pay the bills with tax-free dollars. The idea is to let the employee select from a menu of benefit options rather than being limited, as in the past, to what the company serves up. Cafeteria plans provide the best of two worlds and are what you can expect in the future as the boss and the worker get together to beat the IRS. In short, a new wrinkle in the tax code lets employees spend tax-free money where they want to, while employers save a bundle.

"In actual practice the employer takes money, on a voluntary basis, from the employee's pre-tax wages and puts it in a 'reimbursement account.' The funds never show up on a W-2 form. The employee can then withdraw the money, tax free, to pay for expenses not covered by traditional fringe-benefit plans, such as legal advice, the kids' orthodontic work, care of elderly parents, home/auto insurance, and even a live-in housekeeper."

"We don't need the live-in housekeeper," Nancy said, wiping that grin off Bill's face, "but the money for the kids' braces would come in handy."

"Not paying me all this money, yet letting me spend it on regular bills without paying taxes—is that legal?" There was a puzzled frown on Bill's face.

"The IRS claims reimbursement accounts are 'little more than a tax dodge,' and the final regulations aren't in yet," I replied. "But most companies offering the plans believe they're acting within the spirit of the new law and don't expect problems. One employer I talked with asked, 'Why does a single worker need a rich life insurance plan? He can spend his money on other benefits. Otherwise, all he'll end up with when he dies is a rich cat!'"

After Bill and Nancy left that evening, I began to wonder where our tax laws are headed. Inevitably, some people are going to end up with a better deal than others. Like John Thomas, standing in his garden at sunset. I leaned over the back fence and caught John's eye. He's a branch manager of our local bank. The rain had stopped. The bugs were out.

"You know," John said, "I'll save more than $2,000 this year on child care, thanks to our company's new cafeteria plan. It's fantastic," the forty-three-year-old divorced father of three says. "I can't believe the IRS lets me and my company get away with it."

"You're paying bills without first paying taxes?" I asked.

"It's easy," he explained, "I have the company deduct $250 from my paycheck every two weeks, for a total of $6,500. During the year, I submit bills from my housekeeper and they are paid out of the company's child-care reimbursement account. Assuming even a 30% tax rate, I'd have to come up with more than $9,000 to get the $6,500 I need to pay for the kids' care."

"What about using tax-free money to pay for orthodontic work on the kids, even home and auto insurance?" I asked.

"That's what I like about our new cafeteria plan. It lets you choose where your money is going. The plan provides me with credits equivalent to dollar values placed on each benefit option already provided. With these 'credits' I can buy or sell benefits as long as I keep the company's minimum health and life insurance coverage. In a way," John smiles, "it's like a bank. I can trade up for better benefits by using these available credits, or, as I do with the child-care option, I can use my own money before Uncle Sam, the State, and Social Security take their taxes out.

"I've even got the option of trading in some of my benefits for cash, which would be taxed as regular income, or I can put the money into a tax-deferred retirement account."

Today's benefit plans were designed for the family of the fifties, when dad went to work, mom stayed home with the kids. Benefits were limited to what the company served up. Cafeteria plans are designed to accommodate the changing needs of today's work force. That includes a number of items rarely seen in benefit plans of the past—benefits that work for the increasing number of single parents and two-career families with young children. If you're going to stay ahead in the money game, you need to look at the revolution that's occurring in your employer's fringe-benefit package.

In other areas, in an Alice-in-Wonderland situation, Congress is cracking down on the free ride when we pay our own insurance and benefit bills and prudently save for retirement, but then, at the same time, it's opening the tax-free floodgates with cafeteria plans where we work.

To stem the rush into company-provided fringe benefits, another idea is floating around Congress. That's the possible taxation of company-provided fringe benefits.

Taxation of Fringe Benefits

Currently you don't pay income taxes on the insurance premiums paid on your behalf by your employer. The present administration believes, however, that paying income taxes on these fringe benefits would generate several billion dollars of revenue and help control health costs, which have been rising twice as fast as the Consumer Price Index. Taxing part, or all, of the employer's contributions for medical and dental benefits could also apply to long-term disability.

Life insurance already is taxable to some extent, and you should take care when your employer offers you more "free" life insurance as part of the company's group life plan. In fact, group life insurance from your employer can become a costly fringe benefit. Currently, you aren't taxed on employer-paid group term insurance until your coverage exceeds $50,000, but your company's premium for any coverage above that amount is taxable income to you. Years ago the IRS ruled that when you receive life insurance protection provided solely by the employer's contribution, you receive an "economic benefit" and that benefit is includable in your gross income at the end of the tax year.

The amount of the additional income based on your excess coverage over $50,000 will be included in your federal income tax return. You should also check your state law. Some states may set limits even lower than $50,000. The federal limit of $50,000 applies to the aggregate coverage from all employer- or job-related paid group plans.

To help you calculate your own "reportable income," here's a copy of the Uniform Premium Table. Your age for this table is your attained age on the last day of the taxable year.

Uniform Premium for $1,000 of Group Term Life Protection

5-Year Age Brackets	*Cost Per $1,000 of Protection for One Month Period*
Under age 30	$ .08
30-34	.10
35-39	.14
40-44	.23
45-49	.40
50-54	.68
55-59	1.10
60 and over	1.63

Suppose you're a fifty-year-old male with $150,000 of group life insurance paid for by your employer. Using the Uniform Premium Table, your additional income is:

Excess coverage over $50,000 .... $100,000.00
Annual cost per $1,000 @ .68 cents x 12 .... $8.16
$100,000 x $8.16 per $1,000 = ... $816.00

Any contributions you make for the group life insurance may be subtracted from the amount derived from the use of the Uniform Premium Table. You can escape taxation completely if you are retired for age or disability, or if the beneficiary is a charity.

Let's look at your real cost. Because the IRS figures your cost for benefits over $50,000 from an arbitrary table long out of date, you may be getting "free" life insurance at a loss. The new low-cost term rates now offered by major life insurance companies for healthy applicants compare with the government's Uniform Premium Table like this: At age forty-five, premiums for individual policies can be about half the government table; at age fifty, about one-third that cost; at sixty, about one-fourth.

Inflation has skyrocketed the free life insurance most of us receive with the job. It now costs most people more to take the added "free" insurance than to get a taxable pay raise equal to the group premium and to buy their own insurance. That's because individual premiums have fallen so low that, in many cases, they are less than the taxes you'd have to pay for the free insurance from the company. One person I know refused an additional $150,000 of added group insurance, bought his own, and saved about $380 a year.

Separating fact from emotion, inflation and high-interest rates tell us today that life insurance we get from our employer—or that which we buy on our own as term insurance—is a security blanket to wrap around our dependents if we die today, not necessarily an investment for our old age.

The advantage to buying your own life insurance is, not only can you often do better than the free, company term policy, but you can keep the insurance whenever you change jobs.

Vesting

Have you ever wondered why it's so difficult during your working years to keep your retirement assets in one place? Just look at all those ads offering you a higher salary and a fantastic career if only you'd change jobs. It's an appeal to greed, and it wins. From a nation that once gave away thirty-year service pins in clusters, we have moved to a nation where men change jobs, on average, every four-and-a-half years, women every three.

Understanding vesting could be the most complicated part of this book. The problem with vesting is that Congress makes up the rules. Most books that explain retirement plan vesting have trouble with the English language. Vesting, in simple, nonpension language, means your right to receive your employer's contribution, with all its earned interest, when employment is terminated prior to retirement. It also means you can lose as much as $50,000 to $100,000 in retirement benefits during your working years, ripped off by a system that's geared to favor the boss. Ultimately it means that, for most of us, any chance of a work-related retirement income is not in the cards because the company is holding all the aces.

When can you be affected by vesting? When you:

Retire under the company plan;

Become disabled and unable to work;

Leave your present employer;

Have enough years of service with the employer.

In a nutshell here's how vesting works: Once you are covered under your employer's retirement plan, you begin to earn fractional vesting credits. That's the term your employer uses to let you know that some, but not all, of his contributions to your retirement account may belong to you. The amount of vesting you actually have during any given year will depend on the number of years you've been in the plan and the vesting schedule used.

Retirement plan vesting is something like falling into an icy river; you're too numbed to do anything, yet it's too cold to stay in the river. But vesting schedules don't need to set your teeth chattering. To tell the truth you're never going to change the system, but you can understand when the danger signals start ringing. Let's look at why we have vesting in a pension plan.

Vesting helps employers pay their bills. By keeping your right to vesting low, or nonexistent, during the period of high employee turnover (usually between the first and sixth year of retirement plan coverage), companies have been able to stave off a continued cash drain. They can use their pension contributions for not just one employee, but for several. That's because the money you leave behind when you change jobs before you've been with the company long enough to earn 100% vesting (usually ten years) drops immediately into the boss's pocketbook. For example, suppose you have $5,000 in your pension account, and you are 30% vested when you pick up your last paycheck. You'd get $1,500 (30% of $5,000), and the balance, $3,500, stays in the pension plan to reduce your employer's future cost.

For the boss, it turns out to be a happy goodbye. For cash starved pension plans across America, struggling to remain alive during this prolonged recession, it's a godsend. For most American workers, it's a disaster. If you want to stay ahead in the money game, you'll need to learn how to keep from being ripped off when you change jobs.

That's important, because vesting schedules used in our nation's retirement plans vary to such an extent that under one pension plan you could be 40% vested after four years and under another plan you might not be vested at all. But you can fight back—and protect your vesting rights.

The answer to getting the best deal on the money your boss has put under your name in the company retirement plan begins with the least-read book in the country. Like *The Repair and Maintenance of the Edsel,* it's not a book for everyone; yet it touches the

133

lives of some 80 million workers and their families. It's not an easy book to read, yet its action-packed chapters can bring financial catastrophe to the unwary. In the lingo of retirement, it's called The Summary Plan Description booklet. The rules say it should be written in easy-to-understand, plain English and should help you understand how your retirement plan works. Your employer (or your personnel office) must give you a copy of the *Summary Plan Description* booklet when you join the company's retirement plan, or any time you request a copy. That's the law.

If you want to step out in pursuit of all the money your employer has locked up in your pension account, you'll need to study the vesting schedule and learn how it works. Try to calculate your current vesting, based on the number of years you've been covered under the plan. (This may not be the same as the number of years you've been with the company, since you'll usually have to wait at least a year, sometimes up to three years, before you're eligible to join the plan.)

Two other tips to remember as you read the booklet:

● Determine the anniversary date of your retirement plan—when the plan's year ends. This is usually at the end of the company's tax year. This is usually at the end of the company's tax year. The date can be important if you have a choice when you leave the company because, if you work beyond the plan's anniversary date, you may get credit for another year of vesting. This could mean going, from say, 60% to 70% of all the money in your pension account, including the most recent contribution made at end of the retirement plan year.

● Once you leave your employer and receive the money from your company's retirement plan, you have only sixty days to roll over part, or all, of the cash into your own roll-over IRA, to avoid current taxes. There's a fortune wrapped up in your company retirement plan if you decide to let it continue to grow tax-deferred until you retire. (Refer to roll-over IRAs in chapter 5.)

Group Hospital/Medical Plans

When you work, full medical insurance is now required up to age seventy. Under a little-known section of the Tax Equity and Fiscal Responsibility Act of 1982, employers are now required to cover employees over age sixty-five and their dependents up to age seventy. After age seventy, the employer's insurance will pay only 20% of the claims.

If you, or someone you know, continues to work past age sixty-five, be sure to take advantage of the complete health insurance in your employer's plan; it's the best coverage you can get at a time when you or your dependents will need it the most. The law bars employers from cutting younger workers' benefits to offset higher cost for older staffers. It's an important change in the law that you should plan on using, when you qualify.

Extension of medical benefits for dependents of deceased employees is a new and growing fringe benefit. Many group plans now provide a twelve- or twenty-four-month extension of medical benefits, without premium payments, for the spouse and dependents upon the death of the insured employee. Check to see if your plan offers this benefit, and, if not, why?

401(k) Cash or Deferred Plans

Most people don't like drying dishes any more than they like paying taxes. Neither is much fun. The dishwasher solved the former, and 401(k) plans are rapidly solving the latter. Called "Cash or Deferred Arrangements" under Section 401(k) of the IRS Code, these plans allow you, with the help of your employer, to defer a big chunk of your current income taxes. If you're offered a chance to participate, or if you own your firm, you'll find a lot to like. In 1983, a survey of two hundred clients of a large employee-benefit consulting firm determined that 70% of those surveyed were planning to initiate—or at least study—a cash or deferred profit-sharing plan. Large corporations where 401(k) plans have been offered have experienced an 80%+ participation! In a money game where individual workers are stuck with $2,000 of tax-deferred income in an IRA each year, 401(k)s look like a magic wand.

In a nutshell, 401(k) plans offer employees the opportunity to receive part of their salary, bonus, or profit-sharing distribution either in cash or in the form of a contribution to a tax-qualified plan where it will accumulate, tax deferred.

Why are 401(k) Plans so attractive? Like IRAs, they let you tax-defer money from your paycheck and allow you to save with the magic of tax-deferred compound interest. But from there on, the scale starts to tip in favor of the 401(k). For starters, employees can contribute to 401(k) plans through voluntary salary reduction plans. For example, if you earn $30,000 and you contribute 10% of your salary to a 401(k) plan, your taxable income will be reduced to $27,000. For tax purposes, your $3,000 contribution to the plan will be deemed to be an employer contribution to the plan on your behalf.

The kicker to all of this: Your wages, as reported on your W-2 form, would not include contributions made under a voluntary salary reduction 401(k) program. Unlike any other savings plan, you can save income taxes, many state taxes, and—believe it or not—Social Security (FICA) taxes if your wages are below the FICA wage base. *One hundred percent of the salary or bonuses you defer goes into your savings account.*

The boss likes 401(k) plans, too. The company may save Social Security, workmen's compensation, and unemployment insurance payments, to the extent your pay is reduced for contributions into a 401(k) plan. What's more, the salary you defer is deductible by the company as a contribution to the retirement plan.

If you are, as I am, a confirmed dime pincher you may be amazed how 401(k) plans allow the IRS income tax rules to jump the rails. A $2,000 limit with IRAs is now small potatoes. Contributions to 401(k) plans are subject only to the same limitations that apply to any profit-sharing plan. Subject to antidiscrimation rules, you could theoretically defer as much as 25% of your compensation, or $30,000. But, as a practical matter, a rule about aggregate deductible contributions will normally lower your contributions to 15% of your total compensation.

In our example, the individual who earns $30,000 could defer up to $4,500 into a 401(k) plan. I have never quite grasped the idea of letting so many people sidetrack the IRS by using something as weird as the numbers 401. Taxes, for God's sake, are what everyone pays to run the country. Everyone's fair share includes everyone paying the same rate. But 401(k) plans let you jump the tax rails again. With a 401(k) plan, you can also make up to a $2,000 contribution ($2,250, if one spouse is not employed outside the home) to your IRA. Jumping back to our example again, the individual with the $30,000 salary can now bury up to $6,500— $4,500 with the 401(k) plan and $2,000 with an IRA. Two-income couples could defer taxes on $8,500. And the IRS can help you save big dollars for the future, too!

In a one-third tax bracket, with a $6,500 contribution from your pay, you could save about $1,490 on federal income taxes and more than $300 on Social Security taxes! That's a whopping $1,800 a year just because the employer allowed you to crawl through the 401(k) loophole.

But with the magic of tax-deferred compound interest, that $1,800 saved in taxes can make a big difference in whether you ever accumulate enough dollars when you start to live on mailbox checks. Here's why. That $1,800 inside the tax-qualified, tax-deferred plan saved each year, earning a constant 11%, can grow to $33,450 in ten years. At the end of only fifteen years, saving this $1,800 from the tax office each year, your "extra cash" account can soar to about $69,000. That's money you would not otherwise have, without the magic of 401(k).

With the 401(k)s, you have yet another tax break when you take the money out. With most tax-favored plans, what goes in tax deferred must come out some day with a big tax liability. The IRS is patient, but rarely forgetful. When you make withdrawals from an IRA, they are taxed as ordinary income, yet 401(k)s allow lump-sum distributions with the special tax-favored, ten-year income averaging. Again, another often overlooked advantage of tax-deferred savings is the special tax treatment when you take out the money. For our lucky 401(k) saver, the results can be startling. A $100,000 lump sum distribution from an IRA to a participant in the 40% tax bracket would result in current income taxes of $40,000. For the same withdrawal from the 401(k) plan, the special ten-year averaging reduces income taxes to about $15,400.

If you already feel unequal by a supposedly equal tax law, you are right. Finding out about 401(k) plans and not working at a place where you can have one is like finding out about a free trip to Europe that applies only to the people who work upstairs. It hurts.

Here's another gem. The 401(k)s dangle the bait of no-penalty tax when you take out the money. You can get your hands on the money in a 401(k) plan without penalty on retirement, *when you leave your employer* who is offering the 401(k) plan, at death, disability, or after age fifty-nine and a half, whichever comes first. In addition, since 401(k) plans are like company-paid retirement plans, withdrawals can be made for "hardship," which has been stretched to include such basic needs as college tuition or a down payment on a home. And if you need money to remodel your kitchen, take a vacation to Pago Pago, or buy that Mercedes you've always craved, you might be able to borrow the money from the 401(k) plan if certain conditions are met. And you can do all of this with money on which you've yet to pay a penny of tax!

One of the reasons 401(k) plans remained one of the best-kept secrets of company employee benefit managers is that employers faced administrative problems with them not encountered in other retirement plans. The other reason is that, until 1982, the IRS had not clarified its position on proposed regulations that allowed companies to set up 401(k) plans. These regulations require that plans pass a nondiscrimination test. In its simplest form, this requires that the highest-paid one-third of all employees not contribute more than 1.5 times the amount contributed by the lower-paid two-thirds.

The employer must set up and administer the plan for the benefit of all employees. Many insurance companies, mutual funds, brokers, and some banks offering 401(k) plans say that cost savings can actually pay for the start-up and salary reduction costs. (The Scudder Funds in Boston, for example, has complete adoption agreements, prototype plan, and trust agreement to establish a 401(k) plan; and they will do the plan administrative services for a "hands-off" approach to the world of 401(k).) That's because the employer saves a great deal of money when you defer part of your salary into a 401(k) plan. With the deferred income no longer on the books as salary, the company saves on Social Security payments, workman's compensation, and unemployment insurance. On Social Security, running about 7% of payroll, our example of a $4,500 contribution to the 401(k) plan could save the company $300 a year. That's a powerful incentive for the boss to let employees bypass the IRS!

As we've said, 401(k) plans must be established by the employer. If your company does not offer this type of plan, ask why not and see what you can do to get one started. Most financial and retirement planners believe tax-deferring plans like 401(k) will become a "must" for working people who want and need the larger deductible amounts and flexibility that IRAs do not provide.

The message delivered in this chapter is that many of the ways you'll use to stay ahead in the money game in the decade of the eighties will be found in the magic of fringe benefits. In that world of tax-free and tax-deferred money you can fix crooked teeth, pay the bills for an older parent, borrow money to send a child to college, and legally avoid paying taxes on amounts three or four times greater than the other "worker's loophole," the IRA.

Even more important, by looking closely at the tax codes that apply to your employer's fringe benefits and retirement plans, you can save a bundle of cash you would otherwise pay in taxes. That's the money you can save—often without taking a penny out of your current living expenses—that can make the difference when you retire.

PART TWO

PART TWO

INTRODUCTION TO PART TWO

In the following chapters I want to help you build your own financial plan and to give you some practical advice on how to work out your own financial strategy. I'll outline what I believe can work for you depending on your life situation, your age—and your personality.

What's important to remember about any financial book is that our attitudes on saving and investing money vary widely. How we feel about money is often influenced by the turbulent economic times that shaped our particular generation. As a result, the way we handle money today often depends on how much of it we had while we were growing up. That's why I'll break down the financial planning into three different generations: the free-spending younger generation, the solid middle years after the children are grown, and the retired generation.

Within each generation there are conservatives, risk-takers, and middle-of-the-road types. Your job is to determine where you fit, your comfort zone, because how you feel about money can be more important than what you do with money. Translation:

Most people tend to be aggressive investors in their early years. The better the salary and income potential, the more speculative the investments. This can mean investing in start-up or high risk companies, precious metals, or real estate. In the conservation years, out goes the risky stuff. The idea at this stage in life is to conserve and build a strong financial base, most likely including a home, with savings and investments offering a solid growth potential. In retirement, the emphasis shifts largely to income-producing assets to replace lost wages. The idea is to produce as much income as you can without touching the principal, since most retirees worry about running out of money before they run out of breath.

If you want to chart your own financial course, make your own decisions, and be responsible for your own future, you can. Independence, however, can carry a high price tag. Most of us, captives of a tightly controlled system where financial institutions offered identical investments and savings plans, have never had any real opportunity to manage our own money.

But today, with financial deregulation rolling across the landscape, banks, nonbanks, and near-banks pour out a constant array of new investment and savings plans. Why, Sears Roebuck, on any given day, can sell you a set of wrenches, an insurance policy for your home, a sack of grass seed, or ten shares of IBM or AT&T. In short, charting your own financial course today will require more study, more savvy about financial matters than ever before. With new savings and investment products rolling out in the newspapers every day, you'll be forced to choose not only how you want to put your money to work, but with whom.

The good news is that we now enjoy a respite from inflation and, as savers, high, and in many cases double-digit, interest rates and unprecedented opportunities to save and invest without government regulations.

As you read the following chapters on financial planning, keep in mind what I consider the three most important guidelines you'll need as you work out your future security:

- Where you save and invest should make you happy. You've got to sleep at night without nightmares.
- Invest your time *before* you invest your money. Brainstorm your financial moves, find out from your financial institution as much as you can before you commit yourself.
- And remember above all else, no one stock has to be bought, no one savings plan has to be opened. There is always another stock or savings plan and always another day.

7

THE BUILDING YEARS:
MAKE MEGABUCKS, SPEND MEGABUCKS

Born after World War II, young American adults in their thirties today belong to the best-educated generation in America's history, yet across the country over 70 million of these men and women— nearly a third of our current population—are scared. These are the children of the postwar baby boom, and the optimism they knew growing up in the sixties and early seventies has been dimmed by problems of getting and keeping jobs, getting ahead.

As they raise their families and establish their careers in the eighties, they are captives of the excesses of the seventies. They face a cost of living that has tripled since the early seventies, making it necessary for both spouses in well over half of all young couples to work today. Even though they earn $50,000 or $60,000 together— what they used to think rich people made—they find that after taxes their income will neither meet their expectations of the good life nor permit them to save for the future.

Most baby boomers are, nevertheless, living the American dream. Better educated and earning far more money than their parents, they face the central problem of how to pay for their current living costs and still save for the future. They grew up in the plentiful fifties and sixties, and their aspirations for the future were often formed by the prosperity of their parents during a time we now remember as an exceptionally optimistic period in American history. The baby boomers who are now in their middle years expected the best education to be followed by rewarding careers; they expected to be prosperous and to have happy, fulfilled family lives.

The reality is that the value of a college degree has dropped. Smokestack industries have turned into computer chips, forcing a relearning of skills, and, in part because of this generation's over-supply in numbers, unemployment has gone up. The basic problem, often overlooked, is that while the baby boomers in their middle years are earning incomes as high as—or even higher than—any preceding generation, their real spendable income, adjusted for inflation, will buy far less. Not only will their incomes buy less, but they face the unhappy prospect of giving a greater share of their paycheck to the tax man. A worrisome prospect indeed.

Another trend gathering momentum is the shift in America from a male-dominated society to a much more androgynous one. It's not that we're switching from a male to a female society; in this society male and female contributions are much more balanced. With over half the working-age women already in the work force, with more two-income couples than one, this trend is causing a profound effect on the business world. In just one generation, the lifestyle of the American woman has shifted from the home to the office. Women have become much more assertive in demanding better job opportunities, and, with better jobs, salary equality for comparable work.

What's more, in a complete break with the traditional dominating male role in business, about a third of the exploding number of new companies rushing into the marketplace are being started by women. Because of the tremendous strides made by women in boosting their job opportunities and pay, many married couples today are finding that two incomes can put them into the $50,000, $60,000, or more salary range.

The good news is that we're living in an extraordinary time. In the fifties and sixties, during periods of great stability when everything had a name and a place, the individual didn't have much clout. Society was content to rumble along without moving away from the center line. But in times of great changes, the individual's power and influence on society can be enormous. Where deregulation is sweeping away much of the established order, men and women who can develop a sense of where they're going can have a real impact on the future. That's because the future is cloudy and unpredictable as we make a radical break with the past. For those in their younger years, just getting started in their life's work, the opportunities are just unbelievable.

Most experts believe the way we handle money as adults often depends on the family income while growing up. This is borne out as we see the trend for many in their younger years to spend rather than save. Coming out of a decade of exploding inflation that stripped away much of the value of fixed savings, their attitude toward money and the possessions it will buy often makes their parents wince.

For most of the postwar generation convenience is crucial. The blurring of the differences among banks, thrifts, and brokers that has come with financial deregulation is to them the natural course of events. They often have their paycheck directly deposited in their checking account, they use cash-dispensing teller machines on the way to the grocery store, and with prices rising for everything they buy for the first time, they often try to live from paycheck to paycheck. What follows are some specific recommendations for young people, and those with growing families, to get a handle on their own finances and keep control.

Credit Cards and Debit Cards

Credit cards have become an American way of life. But spending before you have the money to pay for your purchases can often lead to mounting interest charges and rob you of much of your purchasing power. In many "easy pay" plans, interest charges can often amount to half of your monthly payment, keeping you hooked to high credit card interest charges.

If you want to stay ahead in the money game, you need to try desperately to avoid interest charges that can easily run over 20% on the unpaid balance. It won't be easy to pay in full each month, but it could be your first step in building a solid financial future.

The debit card is moving from the automatic teller machine to the gas station and department store. In a banker's heaven, everyone would buy everything with a debit card. Their advertisements come right to the point: "A debit card is the convenience of cash without having to carry it." But remember, a debit card is not a credit card; it's just another name for an automatic teller machine (ATM) card.

When you use a debit card your bank or thrift automatically

deducts the purchase from your checking account. If you don't keep up-to-date records, your checks could soon be bouncing all over town. The big disadvantage with debit cards is that you pay on the spot. With a credit card, you have several weeks to pay for your purchases. You have, in effect, a "float" in which you are using someone else's money.

I believe debit cards will grow as more and more financial institutions band together and expand the convenience of having cash without carrying it. Banks are desperate to get rid of the costly paper handling and the free ride between purchases and payment that many bankers and retailers say saps their profit on credit cards. I believe you should stay away from debit cards unless the convenience outweighs the problems you could later have in balancing your checkbook.

Emergency Funds

The first item in building any financial plan should be the establishment of an emergency fund. Most planners recommend at least three or four months of current income be set aside for unexpected financial needs. Sometimes we remain fearful of falling behind in our financial obligations and the presence of our own "bank," ready to come to our aid, is a comforting thought indeed. As with all banks, however, you must take the money out in a prudent way and schedule a repayment system for your personal one-stop financial center.

A good way to begin building, or resupplying, this money center is to ask your bank or savings and loan to take the savings out of your checking account before you can get your hands on it. Building up an emergency fund can be one of the most difficult and painful ways to allocate your money, but in today's uncertain economy it could be one of the most important savings plans you'll ever open.

You'll have to discipline your desire to spend; keep your sticky fingers out of your checkbook when you want something you may not need, just because the money's there. An emergency fund can often make the difference between a good financial plan and one where you just seem to get by.

Knowing how to stay afloat in hard times resulting from the death of a spouse, loss of a job, or a disabling illness can mean the difference between survival and serious financial trouble. Since the Reagan administration has taken a hatchet to the nation's safety net, most Americans have come to rely entirely on company-paid life and disability plans to bail them out of such emergencies. Very seldom, however, do they take the time to find the gaps in these programs or even determine if the coverage the company provides is adequate. Then, in these uncertain economic times, when a layoff or other serious setback hits, they find themselves out in the cold.

Life Insurance

If you need life insurance, buy it for protection. If you're on a tight budget, don't buy a whole life policy that requires higher premiums as long as you live. The stockpiling of this horde of cash won't protect your dependents, and it can substantially cut the amount of death protection you can provide your family. The example from chapter 4, where you can, at age thirty, pay an annual premium of about $1,200 for $100,000 of whole life insurance or buy a term policy for $100,000 and pay about $150 a year illustrates the choice you need to make now.

Maybe what you really need instead of whole life insurance is money to pay off the mortgage and provide for a continued family income. With the cost of term life insurance at an all-time low, I suggest that you try to buy $200,000 or $300,000 of term.

The annual premium should be between $400 and $700. Be sure to check out the new Joint Life policies that cover both spouses and pay the death benefit upon the death of either spouse. By combining coverage the cost is often much lower than for separate policies.

Long-Term Disability

Another area to consider in protecting your standard of living is what has now become known as "silent death." Your life insurance, your salary, your medical policy all fall silent in the face of long-term disability. I urge you to check out your employer's group long-term disability benefits and determine what might be available in the event of your disability. Most group policies don't start to pay for ninety or one-hundred and eighty days after you become disabled. If your employer does not provide this initial benefit, or if you think you need to buy some on your own, be very careful when you shop for long-term disability coverage. During economic recessions and high unemployment many insurers cut back on the benefits they offer. If possible, and if you can pass a medical exam, try to buy your long-term disability protection policy on a medical basis. When the insurance company checks out your medical history and personal habits *before they issue the policy* you can expect far better coverage than if you simply fill out a form and pay the premium. And, of course, once you're disabled, you can forget about purchasing such coverage.

If you have disability coverage at work check to see if it's short-term (usually six months to one year) or long-term (one year or more). Work-related policies also have a maximum payment regardless of your earnings. And remember, you can't convert from a group policy to an individual policy when you leave the job.

Before you shop for long-term disability coverage, contact your Social Security office and ask what disability benefits you'll get. Social Security begins disability payments only after you've been disabled for at least six months. Your state may also pay short-term disability benefits. By adding together these sources of income against your projected expenses, you can get an idea of whether you need to look into buying a policy to bridge any anticipated gap.

When you compare policies, you'll find three generic types of long-term disability insurance. Not all may be issued in your state, but you should find at least one or two.

- Noncancelable and Guaranteed Renewable. This is the best one you can get because the insurance company can't raise your premiums and you, the insured, have the right to renew the policy at the same premiums stated in your policy up to age 65.
- Guaranteed Renewable. This policy is less expensive, but in exchange for lower initial premiums the company can raise the rates. If rates are increased they will apply to an entire class of policyholders, not just for you. You retain the right to renew; however, you may eventually be priced out of the market.
- Commercial. This type of policy guarantees neither the rate nor the right to renew. You can't be terminated in mid-term. Pay your premiums on an annual basis to cut your chance of cancellation.

Today, according to financial planners, only 15 to 20% of their clients—many of whom are well-paid executives—have any personal disability income insurance. If you want to stay ahead in the money game you've got to look at the dangers you face with silent death. As part of your financial planning, figure out where and how you'd get the money you'd need in the event you or your spouse collides with a truck and ends up in a wheelchair for life. It's not a pleasant thing to think about, but neither is a life of silent death.

Buying a Home

Some financial planners believe that working couples and new families might come out ahead today by renting a place to live and building up their assets first. They suggest that you buy stocks, bonds, and commercial real estate. Others believe that homeownership as an investment is being minimized by relatively high mortgage rates and slowly rising home values. Experts in this area like to point out that younger people in lower tax brackets who buy a home may find little tax advantage in paying high interest and property tax.

What these experts often overlook in the numbers and tax game is that everyone needs a place to live, but not everyone has to buy stocks and bonds. My concern, with inflation surging again after the recession, is that the price of your home may rise much faster than what your earnings from other investments can earn. If you need a home, buy it as soon as you can. The psychological satisfaction of owning one's home continues to remain strong. Getting your hands on a place to call home can more than offset whatever you could have made—or lost—in the market.

For most people a home of their own is one of the first major goals in their financial plans. It's also a good example of how inflation has overtaken our ability to save. Many younger people who waited to buy have now been priced out of the market. Prices for single-family homes, on average, have doubled, and in some locations tripled, over the last ten years. And soaring home prices have substantially boosted the money they'll need to save for the down payment. A 20% down payment that used to take $8,000 or $10,000 can now take as much as $15,000 or $20,000. But the real problem many younger couples face is the way taxes shred whatever they save for their home. In fact, if you put the financial numbers down on paper it often becomes technically impossible for a working family to save fast enough to overcome the rising price of a single-family home. For example, suppose a home is $70,000 and rising in price this year about 10%. If you look at a usual 20% down payment, that's a jump of $1,400 in the down payment alone. With two incomes in a 33% tax bracket you'll need an extra $2,000 of income this year just to boost your savings enough to make the rising down payment. That's why if you don't already own a home or condo, try to borrow the money to make the down payment and use the repayment of this loan as a forced saving plan. Remember, when you borrow money—money that you can repay within your comfort zone—you freeze the cost of your home.

A home that promises price appreciation can ultimately become a major part of your financial assets. That's why I believe it's so important for Congress to expand the IRAs to include the opportunity to use these funds as part of your down payment. Since you can save money five or six times faster when you don't pay taxes first, that could well be your key to accumulating the rising down payment you'll need in the years to come.

Retirement Savings

The next item of serious business is starting your retirement savings. You should try to accumulate enough money to replace 75% of your preretirement income. You may want to try to shoot for more, but that's a reasonable level of income in retirement.

HOW MUCH DO I NEED TO SAVE FOR RETIREMENT? A good rule of thumb is that if you can put aside 8% of your pretax earnings each year between the ages of thirty and sixty-five and consistently earn two percentage points more than the inflation rate, you should be able to retire with some degree of comfort. To retire at sixty, you'd need to stash away at least 10% of your pay each year. To make these numbers work out, however, you'll need to see that your money drops inside a tax-favored retirement plan. That's why chapters 5 and 6 can be so important to your long-range savings plan. If you've learned anything about Social Security you already know it's drowning in red ink. The benefits you can expect in the next century will be little more than survival income.

WHEN SHOULD I START TO SAVE? Once you've reached your thirties and you're ready to do some serious money accumulating, it's important to remember the magic of tax-deferred compound earnings. As a general rule, if you start saving the same amount of money in a tax-favored retirement plan at age thirty you'll have almost twice as much money at age sixty-five as if you start at age thirty-five, almost four times as much money as if you start to save for retirement at age forty. In the financial world of the future it's almost impossible to make up for lost time. The good news is that the magic of tax-deferred compound earnings works in reverse. If you save less beginning at age thirty than at age thirty-five, you can end up with about the same pile of cash at age sixty-five. In fact, you can save each year, starting at age thirty, a great deal less than when you start at age forty and still end up with about the same retirement nest egg at sixty-five.

Tax-Favored Savings Plans

It's hard to ignore the importance of IRAs in our long-range financial planning, but if you're young, let's say under thirty-five, and have a couple of children as well as mortgage and property tax payments that take a big chunk out of your paycheck, you may want to think twice about an IRA. That's especially true if you are covered by a retirement plan where you work, plan to stay with your present employer for some time, and you expect to be in a money bind for the next few years. For those of us under forty, the biggest drawback to an IRA is that it locks up our money where we can't get at it without paying a big penalty. For a growing family with growing financial needs, that's a real concern. If you're building up equity in your home and if your employer is making hefty contributions to your company retirement plan, it may be better to stash your extra funds in a more liquid investment, where you can get your hands on the money in a hurry.

IRAs were never designed to serve as a back-up for you in emergencies. If that emergency happens within five to six years of investing in an IRA, and if you have no other ready assets except those in your IRA, you would have been better off to build an emergency fund using taxable investments.

When should you begin to stash your spare cash away in an IRA or other tax-favored retirement plan? This is primarily a personal decision—a trade-off, if you will, between saving money now by paying taxes or saving money later by delaying taxes. When you do start an IRA in your thirties don't think an IRA is forever. The $2,000 you invest this year (or whatever amount you can spare up to $2,000) is not the only investment you'll ever make. Next year you may be able to invest another $2,000, and you may want to open a different IRA somewhere else. Ten or fifteen years from now you may want to combine all of your various IRAs into a single, self-directed account. Until we reach at least fifty, IRAs are nothing more than pigeonholes to park our money and delay the taxes on both the original investment and earned income.

You should, however, expect to reexamine your IRA investments regularly and to change IRA investments several times before you retire.

When you open an IRA be sure to look at the fine print. Once opened, IRAs tend to become old friends, yearly places to plunk down part of our savings for retirement. But every IRA has special features. Most have fees, maturities, costs, and some have their own withdrawal penalties. Figure out what benefits you'll get before you plunge in. I would suggest that you invest in some no-load growth stock mutual funds, and some money market funds that are designed for IRAs. Some high-income funds offer a startling three or four percentage points more interest than FSLIC-protected savings plans offered by a thrift. Minimum investments can be as low as $100 so you can begin on a monthly basis, but stay with a large, well-known fund because its name can help to guarantee the safety of your funds. Whatever you invest in, remember it's the pre-tax yield that's important.

The reason I favor no-load investment funds or money market funds is that should you become trapped in a money bind in a few years and you desperately need the cash, you can withdraw your money without an interest penalty, although you will still have to pay taxes on it. With a bank or thrift you could face "substantial early withdrawal penalties" when you try to withdraw your IRA cash.

While an IRA may not be the right investment for you today, remember that as soon as you can spare the cash for any type of long-range investment strategy, it should be your first priority. That's because *you can save money five or six times faster in an IRA than you can on your own when you pay your taxes first.*

Job Hopping

The big unseen money loser in your middle years can result from your pursuit of higher earnings and a better job. You change jobs and stroll out the door with a hefty pension or profit-sharing check in your pocket or purse—but you're still a long way from retiring. Yet the temptation to spend some or all of this money can be overwhelming. On the other hand, these funds could be a big part of your retirement nest egg later on. What should you do? It can easily be one of the most frustrating decisions you can face.

If you want to stay ahead in the money game when you change jobs (or are let go) you need to start your planning well in advance. Find out how to keep from being ripped off when you leave your employer. That's because when you change jobs you could lose much of the money your employer has contributed on your behalf into the company's retirement plan. It's not that you shouldn't consider changing jobs. The bright lights of new opportunities often shine brilliantly and lead the way to new advancements in job satisfaction and income. What you have to do is consider carefully how you can take with you as much of your employer's prior contributions to your retirement plan as possible.

We're not talking about nickels and dimes. You can lose as much as $50,000 to $100,000 in future retirement benefits during your working years, ripped off by a system that's geared to favor the boss, as was pointed out in chapter 6.

If you are thinking about changing jobs, look at your retirement plan's vesting schedule. Find out for yourself (from reading the pension book your employer will give you if you ask) what your vesting level is (the percentage of the money in your retirement account that is earned and which you can take with you when you leave the company's retirement plan) and ask your employer for a lump sum payout. Some employers will try to keep the money in the retirement plan until you retire, offering to pay you a monthly income when you pass the plan's retirement age. If you can get your hands on the money when you leave you'll accomplish two important things: you won't have to locate the company's retirement plan at retirement and take the monthly payout the plan offers and, in all probability, you can manage the money better on your own than if you left it with the employer. In this period of recession, you might even find you've overcome another problem now facing thousands of employees: the employer's bankruptcy.

Once you get your hands on the money, consider the tax consequences that complicate the matter. Uncle Sam will get his mitts onto some of that cash one way or another, sooner or later, and how much he gets now will depend on what you do with it. And that's the catch. If you take the cash and run, the IRS offers you a nice tax break, something called ten-year forward-averaging. That makes the tax bite less painful than if it were classed as ordinary income, but you'll need to make sure you qualify for ten-year income averaging. It's not automatic. The tax code is jammed full of exceptions and restrictions and this time the IRS may have outdone themselves. Two important conditions for the favored tax treatment are that you receive the entire balance from the retirement plan in one taxable year and that you've been in your employer's plan for at least five years. Remember, the tax rate for ten-year forward-averaging is based on the amount you receive from the retirement plan, not your income as of the moment. An example of the tax would be about 8% on $25,000, 12% on $40,000 and about 14% on $50,000. In general, the smaller the lump sum, the lower the tax rate.

To find out if you actually have a "bona fide lump-sum distribution" from your retirement plan and if you qualify for the tax break, see your accountant or tax advisor.

In any case, with twenty-five or thirty years of tax-deferred income before your retirement, don't take out the cash, pay the taxes, and try to invest in the market in the wild belief that you can do better outside a tax-favored IRA or other retirement plan. You can't.

Unless you need the money for personal living expenses, or you decide to shoot the wad on something you've always wanted—like a boat—roll the money over into a rollover IRA.

Suppose you only want to take out enough money to buy the boat? You've had that pair of special nonslip deck shoes waiting for a chance to feel the waves pounding against a boat for years. Alas, Uncle Sam is no boatman. If you split your lump sum, the part you take in cash is taxed as ordinary income, at regular tax rates. Equally bad news is that the money can also throw you into a higher tax bracket.

Other key points to consider:

Your prior contributions to the employer's retirement plan are not eligible for rollovers because they are not subject to income tax. You already paid the tax when you put the money in the plan. Only the earnings on those contributions are subject to tax and should be rolled over.

If your company is the one to terminate your pension plan and you wind up with a lump sum distribution, you're not eligible for the ten-year forward-averaging break. It's all ordinary income in the year you receive it—unless you roll the lump sum over into your IRA or Keogh plan.

The money you roll over does not have to go into one account. You can put some of the cash into a mutual fund, some into a stock fund or a savings plan.

One more thing is important. You need to watch the calendar while you're mulling over your options. That's because you only have sixty days after you get your hands on the cash from your employer's retirement plan to roll over the money into your roll-over IRA and defer the taxes. If you're unsure what to do, roll over the money into the IRA and think about it. That way you can still get your hands on the money without a tax penalty until you file your tax returns. It will give you time to determine just how much of the cash you'll need for current expenses and how much you can put away in your IRA. If you watch this one point and capture as much as you can of your retirement plan's lump sum payout when you change jobs, you can significantly boost your future retirement income.

It's like letting the boss pay for a good part of your IRA investment. How much are we talking about? Suppose when you change jobs you're thirty-seven and your lump sum distribution is $9,000. If you roll that amount over into an IRA and earn today's high 11% interest for the period, you'd have about $170,000 at age sixty-five. About $100,000 at age sixty.

In spite of what anyone might tell you, there is almost no way in today's financial market that you can do as well by paying your taxes and investing the money on your own. If you are in a 33% tax bracket and you earn the same rate of interest on the $9,000 in a taxable investment, locking it up for the same period of time, you'd have about $35,000 at age sixty-five, only about $25,000 at age sixty! Most small investors fail because in their rush to get their hands on the money, pay taxes, and invest, emotion prevails over common sense. The eternal truth for any investor today is that if you don't first try to save taxes, to tilt the odds in your favor, you can't possibly stay ahead in the money game, or accumulate enough money to retire in style.

Saving Vs. Investing

Most financial experts and I agree on one thing: basics come first. That includes saving for an emergency, adequate life and disability insurance, and owning a home. Then comes tax-deferred savings where you can get Uncle Sam to help you build up your nest egg. Two-income couples, for example, often end up being taxed at the top rates, eroding their ability to sock away money for the future. That's why its so important to remember to save taxes first. Under our current tax laws almost no investment can overcome the money you lose when you pay your taxes first and then invest.

Once you have these important points under control and have increased your disposable income to allow for vacations and the fun side of life, you are ready for some serious financial planning.

To get your hands on the kind of serious money you'll need to save and invest, you have to master the discipline of regular saving. If you wait to save what you have left over at the end of the month, you may end up saving nothing. You need to consider savings as a regular expense in your budget.

If you're going into your thirties, your best move could be to diversify. To plot a basic financial strategy to build your golden nest egg, you should remember the difference between savings and investments. The advertisements that pour out of banks, thrifts, and money market funds urging you to open a savings account want to help you accumulate cash. The interest you earn is your only reward for letting other people use your money. If inflation rises or you're trapped in a long-term, fixed-rate savings account when interest rates soar, you lose. During periods of rapidly compounding inflation, you can actually lose a great deal more in purchasing power than the interest you earn on your account.

Savings accounts are primarily for accumulating short-term money. Saving for a vacation, for something you might want to buy during the next couple of years and for which you'll need readily available cash. Or for that first item in any financial plan, an emergency fund. Savings accounts, by and large, don't provide the important long-term objectives of growth and tax savings. A house, for example, is a long-term investment that promises price appreciation and tax savings. A savings account can only promise to someday return your original deposit and your accumulated interest income.

An investment usually promises a return on your money and the possibility of appreciation on your assets. A blue chip stock is a good example. Its purchase could provide current income from dividends and the expectation of a rise in the price of the stock.

Investments are a way to lay the foundation for your financial future.

At this stage in your life don't borrow to invest in individual long-term investments. The only time you need to borrow money to invest is for your security umbrella, your home. Up until your late thirties or early forties you are getting set in life and building a family. You can have large basic day-to-day expenses. You need, and you'll spend, part of your disposable income on adequate protection for yourself and your family, an education fund, and a fund for just having fun. Or, you may remain single without family responsibilities and you're ready to risk all.

If you're a No-Risk Personality, regardless of your income, you'll want a stable and conservative approach to investing. If you're a Risk Personality, again regardless of income, you're going to want to build your financial empire in a faster, more adventurous way. As baby boomers, growing up on a steady diet of prosperity without the sobering era of depression and war, many younger and middle-aged people have moved into the fast lane. "Upward mobility" is what it's now called—buying a Datsun 280-Z sports car for $13,000 while their parents continue to drive a 1979 Buick.

Investment Strategy for a No-Risk Personality

One of the first rules of smart money management is to think ahead. In your investment strategy your biggest task will be to plan for a return of rising inflation and, with an economic recovery, higher interest rates.

Within your income range, tax planning for your long-term investments may not pay off. It's better to try to accumulate a solid base of assets. But you do have some opportunities to cut your taxes where the tax code has been changed in your favor. In families where both spouses work, you can now generally exclude from tax 10% of the earnings of the lower-paid partner. The exclusion is limited to $3,000. If you run an incorporated business or a partnership, your spouse can work for you and get the exclusion, but not if you are self-employed operating as a proprietorship. In the latter case, however, your spouse is not liable for Social Security tax.

Watching the calendar can also pay off. If you can hold on to your assets for at least a year before you sell, only 40% of the profit is taxed, for a top effective rate of 20%. Selling earlier means that all profits are taxable at your ordinary tax rate. But on securities that turn sour it's often better to dump them early. That's because, each $1 of loss—from an asset held less than a year—can offset $1 of regular income. On assets held over a year, $1 of loss may net you only fifty cents off your regular income. In either case, you can't offset more than $3,000 in a year. From there on, in subsequent years, the rules get complicated, so see your tax advisor if you run into problems.

I would suggest, to keep within your comfort zone, you plan your investment strategy on a combination of high-yield money market funds and one or more conservative or growth stock funds. Your overall strategy would be to balance these two funds depending on the ups and downs of the financial marketplace. When interest rates are high—over 10% on savings—move most of your assets into the money funds. High interest rates tend to send the stock market lower and your growth potential is greatly reduced.

When interest rates fall and the stock market starts to take off, move back into the stock funds. In many cases you can rebuy more stock than you sold. *Riding down a market is never a profitable way to make money.* If interest rates are low and you think they are set for a sharp rise, you may want to go into the bond funds as well. When and how much of your assets you move from your money market fund to the stock fund or back to the money fund will depend on how you read the trend of the financial markets.

Generally, with a no-risk personality, you want to get the greatest return with the lowest risk. But when you are working with a saving period that can stretch for another 25 years or more, you can afford to take some reasonable risks. I don't recommend, however, that you buy individual stocks. You won't be sufficiently diversified, and you probably won't be able to do enough research to pick the winners. Hot tips may give you thrills, but a conservative strategy will give you dependable profits and income. In mutual funds you can spread your risks, move easily from fund to fund, and stay on top of your investments without staying up all night looking at the market charts and volume. You won't get the big wins, but you won't get the wipeouts either.

For the serious investor with a family to raise, picking a simple investment strategy makes sense. If you can develop a feel for where interest rates are headed and watch your investments, from that standpoint alone you'll do well in the crazy market of the future. Many people in their middle years scheme to steal a jump on the market although they likely could make as much money by going along the straight-and-narrow. With financial deregulation, sky-high interest rates, Third World countries going broke, oil prices soaring and then crashing, there's a lot of volatility in our money system that didn't exist just a few years ago. The rules of how money works have changed. Now that you've been out of school for a decade or so, it may be time to relearn them.

If your (or your and your spouse's) income is over $50,000 a year you may want to consider one of the major broker's cash management accounts (see chapter 3). These accounts can tie together all of your investments, let you save short-term money in their money market funds, and keep track of your taxes in a comprehensive way. Your short-term money can also be held with your broker in three and six month T-bills. They often pay a better rate than insured savings and you free yourself from paying state income taxes.

Whatever investment strategy you choose, be sure it's within your comfort zone. If you don't feel comfortable in individual stocks go into stock mutual funds. Much of what you'll want to consider for your investment strategy is valid for under or over $50,000 of annual income.

I do not recommend that you buy gold, silver, or other precious metals. This is a little early in your life to worry about the economy going to hell in a handbag as you hide coins in your desk for your money of last resort. If gold is purchased at all, in my opinion, it needs to be part of a long-term investment strategy for all-out economic collapse.

Investment Strategy for a Risk Personality

From what my letters and radio callers say, a risk or high-risk personality is someone who is single, or married without children with each spouse working outside the home. If you fit this group you share the honor of being, dollar for dollar, the most taxed individuals in America today. With most, if not all, of your income in paychecks—from which taxes are automatically withheld—you come face to face each payday with the mind-boggling complexity of the current U.S. tax code. Your only hope at year-end is to try to recover whatever you can find when you file your returns.

If you're a risk personality, invest in a home, condo, or other tax-favored investment where you can live and take advantage of Uncle Sam. This is the basic foundation of any investment plan no matter which kind of personality you are. You'll also need a bigger emergency fund than no-risk personalities since the chances are good that you'll be changing jobs more frequently, and some of them won't work out. In today's job market, with fast-changing job skills, you could have periods of unemployment and substantial job-related costs.

If you want to speculate, do it with your own money. Very few people successfully make money using borrowed money. One of the surest ways to "over-risk" is to try to combine leverage with a high-risk market. Options, warrants, and commodities are a good example: you can literally get wiped out overnight. Investing or speculating, you can move only at the speed of the market. A Wall Street friend of mine who traded options and commodities summed it up best. "Buying options or commodities with a small down payment is like walking up to a sleeping lion, grabbing his mane, and kicking him in the rear. The ensuing ride can be thrilling, but in the end you'll get eaten alive."

If you want a higher risk portfolio you might look at stocks in emerging industries, new issues, ones you can put away for a time and hope for the best. If you want to play the whole stock market— not just a few shares of some go-go high flyer, but the *whole* market—you can. Lots of investors are doing it. You can speculate on the rise or fall of the general market and forget about individual stocks that might go up or down. You can buy the new mutual fund, the Equity Income Fund S&P 500 Index. The fund's portfolio includes only stocks used in the Standard & Poor's index of 500 issues. Unlike stock mutual funds, the stocks in the portfolio won't be managed. See chapter 4.

For a risk personality, limited-partnership tax shelters that invest in shopping centers, apartment complexes, and other properties can be one way to ease the tax bite. See chapter 3. The typical limited partnership gives you yearly tax write-offs against your current income taxes and, if successful, capital gains after six or eight years. In addition, you may get periodic cash payments that aren't immediately taxed. Usually the minimum investment is $5,000.

Some tax shelters are different. They are straightforward, high-yielding investments in real estate and producing oil wells. As limited partnerships, they end up in IRAs and Keogh plans, and they make up about 12% of all IRA contributions. There's a certain risk even in these conservative limited partnerships, but for a risk personality they are well within your financial plans. The better ones can provide exceptional payoffs five or six years downstream while paying high interest returns each year.

Before you invest in *any* limited partnership you need to understand that your money will be tied up for several years. If you need to sell your interest you could be in big trouble, almost no one wants to buy a second-hand limited partnership with most of the tax benefits already used. This is a point often overlooked by investors as they rush into the glamour of owning a giant shopping center and putting their money where Uncle Sam can't get it.

If you are thinking about investing in tax shelters other than real estate, be careful. The IRS is shaking a big stick at abusers. Making use of its new power to fight "abusive" tax shelter deals, the IRS can quickly close down the promoters themselves with a court order and then follow through fast with the list of investors. Investors can be open for a personal audit, lose their promised tax benefits, and face stiff late-filing penalties and interest charges. Worse yet, the IRS can let months, even years, elapse after a tax shelter is sold before clamping down on the individual investor.

The first thing you want to do is check out the deal as a money-making business. Will it make a profit? Are the first year's write-offs reasonable? (In a sound tax shelter you should not be able to write off more than 100% of your investment in the first year, often less.) Stay away from the offbeat shelters involving stamp plates, gems, phonograph master disks, and art work, and by all means, get an accountant's advice.

These are sour notes, of course, but keep them in mind. It's better to be careful *before* you invest when you're locking up your money for five years or more.

If you're determined to seek faster action, investigate the scheme and the promoter's record thoroughly before you leap. If the deal smells fishy, back off and learn to wait for another day. Don't think you can fool the one who wants to fool you. For risk-takers the problem is often money itself. They'll argue over fifty cents in a restaurant, yet throw as much as $25,000 or $50,000 to some guy who is selling a financial deal, without batting an eye.

The problem with the small investor in the risk market is that, like all business, the best bets to double or triple in value this year are in short supply. They are known by the people who spend all their lives inside the market, by brokers who follow the market. When the public hears about a hot tip it's usually stone cold. Unless you can get on the "special list" of those investors who are known to make quick decisions, and unless you've saved up at least $20,000 for this fast-paced race for big profits, stay away. The money you risk may be just that: risk.

It is not my intent to turn you away from risk investments, but when you're in your thirties you run the very big chance that your pocketbook could outrace your experience.

8

THE MIDDLE YEARS:
BUILDING A SOLID BASE

At precisely 6:55 in the morning Bruce Boyd arrived at the breakfast table. He had ten years still to go before retirement and, like millions of middle-aged Americans, he was worried these days that inflation would reignite as the country came out of the recession and erode his retirement security by gnawing away at all that he had saved. He glanced at his breakfast.

"With the sky-high price of bacon, don't you think two slices would be enough? And this fresh grapefruit! At this time of year it must cost a small fortune!"

"Everything we eat costs a fortune," Alice Boyd replied.

Scanning the financial page of the morning paper, he observed, half aloud, "This new bank savings account is offering us a much higher interest rate than before."

"Speaking of money," Alice said, "I saw this lovely purse at Hatfield's the other day. It's just what I need for my new white dress."

"My God, Alice, if there's one thing you don't need it's another purse. The closet is jammed full of purses."

"Come to think of it, I could do without it," Alice said, "but I thought it would go beautifully with my new dress when we go out with Bob and Tina Saturday night."

"I want to stay home and watch television like other people. What's this night out of yours going to cost me?"

"We're going out to dinner and then to that new play over at the town playhouse. Bruce, we haven't been out in ages."

"The thing I'm worried about is how to pay our bills. Everything seems to be going up but my salary," Bruce said, "and you act as if we have a bottomless bank account."

"And all you ever do is complain about money."

"I've noticed that you still know how to spend it."

It was the same old bickering and Bruce Boyd hated it. He pulled the papers back in front of his face. As he looked over the financial page again, with its glowing ads for places to save money, he felt as if he'd had more disposable income when he was in college than he did now.

Most of us in our middle years, with ten or fifteen years to retirement, remain captives of our beginnings. The late 1940s marked the end of a sobering era of depression and war. Most of us started out in the tough rebuilding years. It seemed that only opportunity lay ahead. During our first two decades of life, inflation inched up only about 2.5% a year, and a dollar saved was a dollar that would later be worth a dollar. We bought our first house for $25,000 with the money we had saved. This was the era of the GI bill with $500 down and no closing costs as houses sprang up like mushrooms all across the country. Unlike growing families today, this generation could get a four-bedroom, two-bath house with a big backyard in a decent tract for $16,500—with a thirty-year fixed mortgage at 4.5%.

When Bruce was a child, his father had put in long hours and rarely saw his family. When he was not working he was worried about finding enough money to pay the bills. Like so many of us who lived through those times in hard-working homes all over America, Bruce now tends to associate security with money. Many of us have become compulsive savers. No amount of money can give us the security we need to stop saving. No matter how much our passbook says we've socked away, there is always the recurring fear that some money problem may come along and wipe us out.

Our parents were taught by the Depression that both income and assets can disappear quickly. As a result, we tend to save rather than spend, and we're inclined to put a premium on safety.

Banks and thrifts, seeking to lock up our money, throw at us full-page ads that rekindle our urge to save and remind us of the virtue of thrift. And so we continue to hoard our dollars in saving accounts that don't rise with inflation while we yearn for the material possessions we always believed would someday be ours.

Now, with only a decade or so until retirement, we sense that, because of inflation, we may never realize our financial situation. When we shop we gauge our success not by what we bought but by what we saved. Hooked on saving money, we can smell when dollar days are peaking. From across town we can pick up the scent of the sales signs. We tend to consider it a personal defeat if we have to pay full price for anything. We frequently save money at the risk of losing money because we spend it on less expensive items that quickly wear out.

The overwhelming fear in this age group is not having enough money. And so we save and play it safe in the same way we did when we started to save. We accumulate money wrapped up in federal insurance at a bank or thrift and we continue to lose to taxes and inflation.

Survey after survey has shown that how we feel about money depends on how we feel about ourselves and the rest of our lives. If we continue to build up our savings account out of fear that we'll never have enough money, we often fail to keep score. Perhaps we're too busy saving to consider how much we lose in taxes before we save. Perhaps, in fighting inflation, we fail to understand that our savings—no matter how much federal insurance protection—are actually losing the race with inflation and what our money will eventually buy. And we can run an even greater risk in our headlong drive to lock up our money in insured savings: we can fail to enjoy our family and friends.

Working out a financial plan for this generation can be a chancy business indeed. The idea behind the financial plan I am going to offer in this chapter is one that will allow you to take advantage of the unprecedented choice of products that, because of deregulation, have burst on the scene, aimed at helping you hold on to what you already have. I'm not suggesting that you risk all in pursuit of higher returns. I'm not even suggesting that I can explain to you how some younger people with a family can drive a new Lincoln on an income much less than yours. What I am asking you to do is reconsider the value of continuing to save today's dollars using yesterday's ideas.

You're now probably making more money than you ever dreamed possible and, according to the economists, you're going to make a lot more each year before you retire. You could, in fact, easily double or triple your salary by the time you retire. What you need to do, if you're going to stay ahead of inflation, is alter your financial plans to allow for some growth and tax savings, yet protect yourself from loss. That will mean taking some small risks with your money, risks you can control by keeping a sharp watch over your saving and investing plan, while your assets tend to rise at least as fast as inflation.

Most important, of all, when you plan your financial strategy, work within your comfort zone. You may not be able to change the way you feel about money overnight, and that's all right. Maybe you'll inherit some money that can either make you 9% in the money market or let you finish paying off the 7% mortgage on your home. The computer tells you to invest the money, you'll be ahead by 2%, you'll earn more money. Your head tells you to pay off the mortgage. What it means emotionally can often be more important than what it means in dollars and cents. No matter how many financial plans you read, you cannot apply icy logic to every idea for saving or investing money; you must adapt your decisions to the warmth of life experience.

You need to be careful and yet, if you're going to stay ahead in the money game, you'll need to change too—with safety. To tell you the truth, it won't be easy to change a way of saving for the future simply because someone tells you the future will be different from the past. And it won't be easy to talk with other people about money. The American attitude toward money is one of private knowledge; it's generally agreed that it makes sense to conceal one's income from family and friends. In fact, we may be more relaxed about discussing sex these days. From trying to put together answers to all the money problems in the letters I receive, listening to those problems as I travel around the country and on my call-in radio programs, I've designed an overall investment guidance plan for those in their middle years. You'll have to adapt it to your own individual situation, of course, but it could serve as a track to run on as you pull together your financial assets and plan your long-term security.

A Financial Plan for Your Middle Years

TAX-DEFERRED SAVINGS. Your first objective must be to make sure you've explored every opportunity to save on a tax-deferred basis. Every working year you should plan on investing the maximum amount in your IRA or Keogh plan. If only one spouse works outside the home, you can boost your annual contribution to $2,250. Whenever I talk about IRAs on the radio or at a seminar I invariably come face to face with the fact that women who don't work outside the home are shut out of the tax saving program.

The good news is that Congress is about to change the rules and let nonworking wives contribute the full $2,000 to an Individual Retirement Account. Women could then open their own IRAs, based on their husband's earned income, or add to their spouse's IRA and the couple could then save $4,000, just as two-income couples do.

As part of your tax-deferred savings you've got to consider the new *near-IRAs.* Congress wants to expand the IRA program by moving up the maximum annual contribution limit without offer-·ing an initial tax deduction for the savings over the original $2,000 limit. Nondeductible contributions in the new near-IRAs would be permitted only for taxpayers who have already made the maximum IRA deductible contribution. The initial annual amount is $1,750 for each IRA holder.

IRAs are turning out not to be a free lunch in Washington. Congress was told to expect about $4 billion in IRA deductions in 1982 with a loss of about $1.5 billion in revenue. It's now apparent that at least $20 billion worth of IRAs were opened with a loss of $7 billion in tax revenue. The new near-IRAs, by comparison, are expected to cost the Treasury about $215 million over the next three years. To avoid the tag of "budget busting" any new IRA program will have to offer more illusion than reward, more tax deferring than outright tax deducting.

The idea for the new near-IRAs winds back a decade or more to when saving money in an organized plan began. Before IRAs you could save in your employer's retirement plan with voluntary contributions (up to 10% of your salary) after you first paid all of your taxes. The attraction of the early plans was that once you'd paid your taxes and saved your money, taxes could be deferred on income or profits until you took the money out of the employer's retirement plan.

To give you an idea of just how the three savings plans stack up, lets look at the results when we assume you're in a 40% tax bracket, your savings earn a 10% return over the length of the example and you contribute $1,750 each year.

	IRA	Near-IRA	Fully-Taxable
Amount invested	$1,750	$1,050	$1,050
Interest, first year	175	105	105
Less taxes, first year	0	0	$63
Balance, end of year	$1,925	$1,155	$1,092
End of five years	$12,000	$7,150	$6,200
End of ten years	$30,700	$18,425	$14,670
End of fifteen years	$61,250	$36,750	$25,950

The near-IRA plan and the fully taxable savings plan are about the same for the first few years, but they tend to grow in favor of the near-IRA as the years unfold. I don't recommend that you jump into the new near-IRA plan unless you're sure you can get the same inflation-fighting investments that are available in the market. In this example, you could put your hard-earned savings dollars into the near-IRA plan and earn 10% compound interest. I could invest in some good growth mutual funds, pay my taxes, and come out ahead because the assets in my mutual funds could grow faster than the tax-deferred interest you earn in the near-IRA.

Whatever type of IRA or Keogh plan you choose, I recommend that you make your contribution early in the tax year to earn as much tax-deferred income as you can. Check the previous chapter on IRAs and chapter 5 on IRAs and Keogh plans to complete this part of your financial planning.

SALARY REDUCTION PLANS. Salary reduction plans have several advantages over IRAs. You can tax defer larger amounts *and the amount you defer can escape all taxes,* including Social Security and other state taxes. With salary reduction plans you don't have to take a deduction on your tax return; your contribution simply never shows up on your W-2 form as income. Ask your employer about this super way to save money and taxes, and build up a sizeable nest egg with the magic of tax-deferred compound interest. Most of these plans can be traced back to section 401(k) of the tax law. We covered them in chapter 6.

COMPANY THRIFT PLANS. Check to see if your employer offers a *thrift plan.* These plans are growing as a way to boost employee savings. Unlike IRAs or salary reduction plans, thrift plans can't cut your current tax bill; any contribution you make must come from after-tax salary. Under a qualified company-sponsored thrift plan the employer will offer to match your voluntary contributions, dollar for dollar, or maybe one dollar for every two dollars you put into the plan. The limit is usually between 5 and 10% of your salary. The good news is that both your and your employer's money in a qualified thrift plan will continue to earn tax-deferred income until you draw out the cash.

Vesting, or your right to take the employer's cash in your company's thrift plan with you when you leave your job, is usually very rapid, sometimes 100% in only three to five years. Unlike an IRA plan, you can withdraw your money when you need to, and in most company thrift plans you can take out your own money after about a year without upsetting the tax deferral on the earnings. You can often take your money out without forfeiting the company's matching contributions, even if you're not fully vested.

For major financial burdens you should be able to withdraw or borrow against your vested company contributions. Again, unlike IRAs, when you take out the money at retirement, or if you leave the company, you can cut taxes by using the ten-year forward-averaging tax break. One warning: Be sure you know where the money (your contributions and the employer's money) will be invested.

Some employers have set up thrift plans simply to buy their own stock. If your company is buying its own stock so heavily that most of your assets will wind up in the firm's stock, be careful. For most people, however, a thrift plan is like finding money lying in the street—you need to bend over to reach it, but you'll feel like an idiot if you don't.

JOB HOPPING. If you change jobs in your middle years, read the section in chapter 5 about rolling over your lump sum distribution from your employer's retirement plan. With ten or fifteen years to retirement and rushing toward the magic age of fifty-nine and a half where IRA withdrawal penalties no longer apply, you should make every effort to continue to defer taxes as long as you can.

HOME OWNERSHIP. Continue to pay off your home mortgage; the equity you build up can be part of your retirement nest egg. It's a safe place to put your money. If you intend to keep living in your house for the foreseeable future, it doesn't matter whether the price of housing goes up or down.

Most people feel uncomfortable borrowing money on their

home with a second mortgage. In today's unstable economy, it's unlikely you can find an investment that pays enough to offset your costs—and to reduce the substantial strain on the old fear bone that keeps you awake at night. Paying $100 of interest on any new loan makes no sense at all if you're able only to save about $40 in taxes. It's important in your overall strategy to increase your peace of mind, not jeopardize it.

GIFTS TO CHILDREN. Next to buying a house and saving for retirement, one of your big money worries is paying for the children's education. Or, if your children are grown, you may want to help your grandchildren attend the college of their choice. Careful tax planning can cut your cash outlay up to 50%. The idea is that if you give money to your children, interest and dividends will compound at their low or nonexistent tax rate. There are a number of ways to do this, but once you give money to a child there's no legal way to get it back. Most state laws allow the money to be used for schooling, but if you're the parent you can lose the tax break if you spend the child's money on anything that would be an ordinary parental obligation—clothing, food, and shelter at home. You can give each child up to $10,000 a year ($20,000 for a couple when both spouses participate in the gift) without incurring any federal gift tax.

Zero-coupon bonds could be an excellent way to give a gift that might not be needed for several years. Another way that's gaining favor is to lend the child the money. Suppose your son or daughter is going to college and you will have to foot the bill. You could make your child an interest-free loan and shift income taxes from your high tax bracket to their low or nonexistent tax rate. At today's high interest rates, your child could double the money in a little over six years. You might have to come up with more than twice that amount before taxes.

Banks are eager to help. Most will gladly lend you the money if you don't have the spare cash, at perhaps 1½% above the rate on one of their certificates. You in turn lend the money to the child interest free. He immediately buys the bank's certificate, which also secures the original loan to you. Everybody's happy. You get the tax break of shifting taxes from your high rate to your children's low rate and the bank has a riskless transaction and also turns a profit on money that never went out the door.

A word of warning, however, is in order. The IRS has stubbornly tried to call these interest-free family loans "gifts." After losing on the issue for ten years, the case may be headed to a higher court. But tax experts aren't especially worried about the future of interest-free loans as long as you make sure you have invested the money in your child's name and executed a demand note. In many states it may be necessary to set up a trust to lend money to a minor. Before you try to outflank the IRS by giving or lending money to a child, check with your attorney or financial advisor. It's not always as easy as it seems.

SHORT-TERM CONSUMER DEBT. Pay off your credit card debt each month. It makes no sense at all to pay as much as 22% interest on credit card or consumer debt so you can save the money in a guaranteed savings account paying 8%.

Now let's get down to a savings and investment strategy. I've designed one for a no-risk and one for a risk personality. You may fit in between, somewhere between no-risk and risk, maybe halfway risk. In any event, now that you have the maximum tucked away in your IRA, you are going to have to start planning your long-range financial security. For now, we are enjoying a respite from inflation, yet most of us aren't sure stable prices aren't going to disappear, as they always have, to be replaced by higher prices for everything we buy. As savers we now enjoy high—often double-digit—interest rates, well above the rate of inflation. And the profits to be made in the stock market seem to be irresistible. We strain to be optimistic. We can pray that Reaganomics will work, that we'll have a smashing up-turn in the economy in 1984.

But remember, all of these factors probably won't change the way you think about money. If you're a no-risk personality, you'll continue to save in government-protected savings accounts during a roaring bull market. Nothing is going to shake you from the safety of locking up your money in a bank or thrift.

I believe, as we near the start of 1984, that change may be in order. With the uncertainty over a recovery still lingering, with the real possibility of higher interest rates in 1984 from the continued massive federal budget deficits, I would be cautious about the stock market until the recovery is well under way. As for rising interest rates in 1984, I'd stay away from locking up my money in long-term savings accounts. With the number of savings plans already on the market, and the growing number sure to come as financial deregulation continues to unwind, I'd keep my options open by staying

173

short-term. Here's a chance for you to put your own forecast to work and develop your own investment strategy.

Investment Strategy for a No-Risk Personality

You want to achieve the greatest return with the lowest possible saving or investment risk. Your main objective: safety of capital. I'll try to mix that objective with a realization that rising inflation is also a risk. I'll try to do it in such a way that your money can work harder, let you worry less about accumulating money, enjoy life more. Here's where I believe you can start on your overall financial plan.

SAVINGS PLANS. After you've checked every way you can find to defer taxes, the balance of your discretionary money should be saved and invested in ways that make you comfortable. I suggest that you keep about 50% of your cash in easy-access savings accounts. Then I generally recommend some short-term investments. For conservative savers, during times of economic uncertainty, it's better to lock up your money for no more than six months to assure the maximum return with the lowest possible risk. As a no-risk investor in bad economic times like these you should keep most of your money in savings. The time for you to invest is in good times.

One of the safest things to do while you wait out the financial uncertainties is to get the U.S. government to guarantee your money. I like three and six month T-bills. The minimum is $10,000 with multiples of $5,000 above that amount. You can buy T-bills directly from the Federal Reserve Bank, in person or by mail, or you can pay a small fee to your broker or bank. There is no mystery in T-bills; you're buying government debt. The U.S. Treasury's voracious appetite for money to keep the government afloat forces it to the money well every week. In the confused world of money, the government often pays more interest to investors for its bills, notes, and bonds than millions of Americans receive for their hard-earned cash resting in government-insured savings accounts.

With total government debt running well over $1 trillion and the Treasury forced to borrow at least $200 billion of new money each year to keep its financial house from collapsing, there's plenty enough debt to go around. To help the Treasury sop up enough money to keep Uncle Sam in business, the government now allows you to order T-bills by mail for the cost of a twenty cent stamp.

You can get a free booklet, *Buying Treasury Securities at Federal Reserve Banks,* from the Federal Reserve Bank, Public Relations Department, Box 27622, Richmond, VA 23261. Another excellent twenty-page booklet is *U.S. Treasury Securities,* available free from the Federal Reserve Bank, Securities Department, Station K, Dallas, TX 75222.

To order T-bills, you'll have to enclose a certified personal check or official bank check, payable to the specific Federal Bank you contact, for the face amount of the bills. Since T-bills are sold at a discount, you will get a refund check for your overpayment after the regular Monday auction on the date you specify. When the T-bills mature, you collect their full face value.

Your bank or broker can also sell government debt. Many investors like to know what discount they'll be getting before they buy. Also if you buy T-bills by mail you'll lose the interest on the certified check in transit and the overpayment coming back. Banks and brokers usually charge a handling fee of $25 or $50 for T-bills.

You pay no local or state tax, but you do pay federal tax on your income. You can sell your T-bill before maturity in a secondary market, so it has about the same liquidity as an insured money market savings account. Often, by checking the weekly Treasury auction, you can do better with a T-bill than with an insured savings account.

Another place to save is in money market mutual funds that deal only in government securities. Sears, for example, offers a money fund that is invested in obligations guaranteed by the U.S. government and its agencies. It's essentially an insured savings account. There's no fee to buy or sell the fund and no withdrawal penalties. You can even write checks against the money fund. Check out other money funds that invest in government securities. Right now it's a saver's market and you should shop around for the best deal.

GOLD, SILVER, DIAMONDS. I don't recommend that you follow the doom and gloom crowd who advocate transforming your money into silver, gold bars, or diamonds. First of all, that's not a safe way to invest. It's an investment born of fear. Precious metal market expert Charles Stahl, publisher of a newsletter for the heavy spenders in the gold, silver, and platinum commodity markets, puts the individual's purchase of gold into perspective when he says, "The one thing I learned from all my experiences is that gold is the insurance of last resort. It's often the only thing that will buy life in a life-and-death situation. America is the last station on the refugees' train. When this country goes, there will be no place left to turn.

"If you must own gold, convert two percent of your assets, and then pray you never have to use it."*

Second, it's not a good investment if you want to consistently make money on your money. With so many good money-making ideas all over the place the last thing anyone wants to do is get trapped in dead investments. My four dullards to shun are gold, silver, precious metals, and diamonds. When inflation soared to over 14% last year, these were the investments of the worrywarts. With inflation scaled down sharply, many people who followed the gold bugs and diamond promoters into.these speculative investments are now left holding the bag—a bag that pays no interest income while they wait for the chance to recover their money.

The problem, often overlooked, is that the supply of gold, silver, and diamonds is not inelastic. The potential supply of gold is so great that it could moderate any sharp price increase. Both South Africa and Russia, badly in need of dollars, could dump tons of gold on the market and quickly dampen rising prices. A higher price could lead to an immediate start-up of new mine production, which some experts now say is running about 70% of capacity. And the speculators who got caught in the gold fever could be expected to dump their gold at the first sign that prices are rising enough to recover part of their original investment. The experts that I talked with seem to think that gold will hover between the high three hundreds and the low five hundreds an ounce during 1984 and 1985.

If you invest in these commodities, you'll have to consider your state's sales tax, the holding cost, and the extra 1% or so for insurance. Another problem is the growing number of precious-metal firms that are going out of business, leaving many investors with empty hands. As a sales come-on, investors were led to believe that their gold or silver was safely stored in the firm's vault without charge. Often, when the firm failed, the vault was nearly empty.

These precious-metal dealers who sell and then don't deliver

Forbes magazine, September 29, 1980.

point up the fact that firms that deal in gold and silver tend to fall outside the jurisdiction of government regulatory agencies such as the Securities and Exchange Commission or the Commodity Futures Trading Commission. If you invest in precious metals, don't break the two principal rules of safety. Don't leave anything you buy with the dealer who sold you the metal. Pay the extra storage costs if you must, but get your hands on the metal—coins or bars—while you hold your investment. And don't use your investment in precious metals as collateral for a loan or buy precious metals on margin with a down payment.

Having traded in the commodity market, I will pass on this sobering news: The price of gold can go as high as hysteria will carry it, and as a commodity its price can plummet just as fast. Unless you feel comfortable in this highly volatile marketplace, don't buy gold, silver, or precious stones.

TAX-FREE BONDS. I suggest that if you're in a 40% or higher tax bracket you consider investing about 30% of your money in tax-free bonds. In 1982, an almost unbelievable 96% of the newly issued tax-free bonds were bought by individuals rather than institutions. Interest rates for A-rated 20-year municipal bonds have been averaging about 9%. You can buy individual municipal bonds from your broker, but I don't recommend that you go into the bond market and buy tax-free bonds in amounts less than $25,000. The usual amount for a set (five bonds) is $5,000.

Your friends, the smiling people who want to lock up your money at banks and thrifts, your know-it-all uncle, will tell you that moving into bonds can be a chancy affair. It's possible to lose some of your principal. When you buy bonds you run the risk that interest rates may move higher after you've bought the bonds and thus lower the paper value of your investment. If you sell before maturity you could lose some of your original investment.

As I've already said, however, you run a similar risk when you lock up your money long term in a fixed-rate insured savings account. You get back the full amount at maturity, but you can earn far less than the current market rate when interest rates rise. But for every risk there's a reward. If interest rates move lower, and your bonds are not called for redemption by the issuer, you can make money. I believe it's a risk you can take if you're willing to let other professional bond managers handle your money.

The rewards, on the other hand, can be startling. In a 40% tax bracket, a 9% tax-free bond actually earns you 15% before taxes. An 8% insured money market savings account, only about half that. This means, *after taxes*, you can earn 9% with a tax-free bond and only 4.8% with a taxable savings account. It's not what you save that counts, it's what you keep. In our example, you can keep almost twice as much interest income with tax-free bonds. If state income taxes are a concern, you'll need to invest in bonds from your own state.

But making tax-free bonds easy to buy has prompted a stampede. The smart money began rushing into FSLIC-protected tax-free bonds offered by some banks and brokers. Marketed as *Unit Investment Trusts*, they were a group of selected tax-free bonds managed by people who knew the bond market and how to stay on top of the changing interest rates. A loophole allowed these tax-free bond trusts to be secured by a thrift institution's Certificates of Deposit, which in turn were insured by the FSLIC (Federal Savings & Loan Insurance Corporation). The bonds run ten to twenty years, but you can sell your investment in the market, with settlement usually in five working days. Financial deregulation has made the tax-free market worth looking into.

What made these tax-free Unit Investment Trusts so attractive? They were backed by government insurance, they paid higher interest rates than a regular savings account, your money was liquid without withdrawal penalties, and someone else who knew the business managed your money.

You can also earn tax-free money by investing in municipal bond funds. You get a high yielding, tax-free mutual fund made up of high-quality bonds with average portfolio maturity of twenty-five years. There's a $1,000 minimum without sales charges or commissions, and there should be no penalties for redeeming shares whenever you wish. Many of the larger mutual funds offer tax-free funds invested in municipal bonds within one state so that residents are exempt from both federal and state income taxes.

If you're in the 45-50% tax bracket, you may want to consider one of the more popular money market investments: tax-free money funds. Tax-free money funds are extremely liquid. You can get out of your investment quickly. Most tax-free money funds offer the same options as regular money market mutual funds, including check-writing privileges. Tax-free money funds pay less than regular money market funds so you have to check carefully to see if your tax-free interest income is greater than the currently offered taxable income.

Since tax-free money funds are primarily made up of bonds, you can increase your investment yield if you invest in tax-free money funds when interest rates are declining and sell when interest rates rise. That's because tax-free money funds yield more when interest rates are falling because of the notes and bonds that they hold.

With a chance to thumb their noses at the IRS, American savers continue to hunger for tax-free income. What has developed is a new range of tax-free bond investments that make saving money and taxes a lot easier. If you're in a 40 to 50% tax bracket, you may want to consider the newer tax-free bond funds. The admission ticket here is $1,000. Here are some ideas to consider:

INSURED TAX-FREE BONDS. Van Kampen Merritt, Inc., of Philadelphia offers a tax-free trust insured by American Municipal Bond Assurance Corporation (ABMAC). The insurance protects you in the event the issuer of the bonds defaults, but it does not protect you from the market risk in the event interest rates move up or down while you hold the bonds. Municipal bond insurance is spreading, spurred on by the failure of Washington Public Power Supply System and it's ill-fated attempt to build several nuclear plants.

Historically, municipal bonds have proven to be one of the safest investments possible. They are second only to direct obligations of the federal government for continuous payment. If you feel better with this added municipal bond insurance, it could be worth the slight loss of interest income you pay. However, I suggest that you forget it. Most investors will buy into municipal bond trusts or funds that already have a wide diversification against the unlikely failure of a municipal bond issuer, and I don't think the municipal bond insurance is worth the price.

PROTECTION FROM MARKET RISK. Merrill Lynch is offering a new tax-free bond fund that protects your investment against ordinary market risk—the value of your bonds fluctuates, depending on interest rates. This new idea breaks the rules by protecting your principal from a decline in market value on rising interest rates because five New York savings banks have guaranteed to meet redemptions by repurchasing bonds at face value throughout the life of the fund. Brokers who are touting these new protected bond funds say that if interest rates decline significantly the market value of your investment could exceed your initial purchase price, giving you an opportunity for taxable capital gains. In other words, if the face value of your bond falls because interest rates rise after you buy, you can still sell it at its face value. If the value of your bond increases because interest rates fall after you buy, you could get the profits that might occur when you sell.

Merrill Lynch intends to make a secondary market to enable you to sell your tax-free bonds quickly. It's almost like buying and selling stock except that you're looking for tax-free income, not dividends. You can take monthly interest payments or reinvest your income, but the reinvestment program is not backed by the guaranteed redemption offer.

But Protected Bond Funds could be an answer for savers who want to tuck away their money in a safe place, earn tax-free income, and have the liquidity so that if interest rates start climbing again and the savings institutions don't follow the upward trend, they can break out and grab the highest rates. But all this protection comes at a hefty cost. Merrill Lynch's new tax-free bond fund is scheduled to pay 7%—about 2% less than current market rates.

On the other hand, if your money is in a bank or savings and loan, you'd have to earn about 12% in a 40% tax bracket and 14% in a 50% tax bracket to equal the 7% tax free. And that's hard to do with the same safety you can get with a protected municipal bond fund.

CONSERVATIVE STOCK FUND. To diversify your financial plan I would suggest that you begin to invest your remaining assets in a conservative stock mutual fund that invests in blue chip stocks for capital gains and income (dividends). This might set your teeth chattering, but it's the kind of diversification you'll need to learn if you're going to provide some inflation protection in the decade ahead. And you'll be in good company. Money is pouring into stock market mutual funds, with individual accounts of $25,000 and above representing about 50% of all noninstitutional stock fund shareholders.

I recommend that you look at several conservative stock funds, assess the risk and income return, and stay with a big-name fund or broker. Its reputation and track record are your best safeguard. Mutual funds can be tailored to fit each investor. Unhampered by strict government regulations, investment companies have created special mutual funds for such widely differing purposes as saving tax-free money and investing in stocks in high-risk start-up companies—and the variety keeps growing.

You might want to start out with 5 or 10% of your assets and see if you can live with an equity investment that moves up and down in value. If you're comfortable, you can maintain or increase your investment to maybe 30%, moving more of your savings into the equity market. If you're not, you can sell out quickly and put the money back into solid fixed-value savings accounts. In any event, it's one risk that I'd advise you to begin to take as you expand your no-risk personality to fit the decade of the eighties.

Investment Strategy for a Risk Personality

You want to achieve the greatest return with prudent risks. You are concerned about the safety of your capital, but you also recognize that inflation and taxes can gnaw away at the value of your assets unless you strike out in some new forms of investing.

Once you've accepted the idea that some prudent risk is possible, you open the door to a host of new saving and investment products fashioned from the wave of financial deregulation that is splashing against the front door of your broker, banker, and thrift. But, and this is important, once you move away from complete safety and insured savings you have to become actively involved in your financial planning. Don't risk your money in uncertain investments where the risk is greater than a normal market risk—especially if you don't fully understand. Remember, like the stock market where there is always another stock to buy, in investing money there is always another investment to make. Keep your money in your "holding pen" where you can earn interest as you plan your strategy—or spend it on something you enjoy so you can sleep at night.

After you've investigated the ways you can save and defer taxes, and have provided for an emergency fund, you are ready to begin your financial plan. With ten or fifteen years to retirement, I would suggest that you diversify your assets. My suggestions are for general use. You may want to increase or decrease your activity in each area.

SAVINGS PLANS. With financial deregulation pushing new savings plans on the market almost every day, you can choose from a wide range of insured and noninsured savings accounts, money market mutual funds or T-bills. This is money you can get your hands on quickly, money you may need for family responsibilities, for a special investment, or when you trade in your car. It's money you can then replace from your salary in a convenient and easy way.

Because of the unstable economic times and the confusion resulting from financial deregulation, I would keep about 30% of my assets in the best saving plan I could find. Since you can get your hands on these savings anytime, you can also hold this money as a balance against your equity investments and have it available when the economic upturn is fully under way.

One of the best I've found is the new Government Securities Income Fund, GNMA Series, Unit Investment Trust. The trust stashes your money in Ginnie Maes, (Government National Mortgage Association, GNMA), where it is guaranteed by the full faith and credit of the United States. The minimum investment is $1,000.

You should also investigate U.S. Government Securities Mutual Funds. Several good mutual funds invest only in Ginnie Maes, pay monthly dividends, allow check writing and all the other features of mutual funds.

Ginnie Maes (which were covered in chapter 3) are one way the government pumps money into the housing market. But if you think you may want to invest in Ginnie Maes, remember that they are bonds and the payments you receive each month can contain both interest and principal. You can ask that your income be automatically reinvested to save you the trouble of reinvesting the money each month.

As I've already said, when you rush into bonds you'll be warned that if interest rates rise you could lose money when you sell the bonds. That's true, but with something as liquid as Ginnie Maes you can cut your losses very quickly—something you might find difficult to do if you're locked into a long-term savings account. With a risk personality, Ginnie Mae bonds should be a savings plan that lets you sleep at night.

If you're in a 40% or higher tax bracket I suggest that you consider putting a big chunk of your saving and investment assets in tax-free bonds. How you mix up your savings plans will depend on your tax bracket, but you should have about 30% of your assets in liquid form.

There's no point in getting overcomplicated about how savings accounts and bonds work. The important point is that savers are losers if they earn a net after-tax return that is less than the rate of inflation. They are no longer savers, but lenders.

If you knew which way interest rates were going you could become rich buying and selling bonds. The next best thing to do is learn what you need to know about bonds so you can join the smart savers in pursuit of substantial earnings in the current market. After all, a 40 to 50% *increase* on your savings dollar is worth looking into.

STOCK MARKET. To diversify your assets I suggest that you consider putting the balance of your money, about 60%, into stock mutual funds. For a higher risk, you may want to put 40 or 50% into the equity market and 10 or 20% into real estate partnerships or start-up companies. This could give you an overall balance in fixed savings, the equity market and higher risk investments.

I don't recommend the purchase of individual stocks for part-time investors. If you go into the stock market as an individual investor you will learn that it's a market where greed wins and fear rules. That's why most of us don't have the temperament to succeed. The eternal truth about the market is that you must buy when prices are low and everyone is discouraged. You sell when prices rise and everyone wants to buy. The rest of the time you sit on the sidelines and wait. Robert Rhea, Dow historian and stock market guru, summed it up best: "Any person who tries to be in the market at all times is almost certain to lose money, for there are many periods when even the most skillful trader is in doubt as to what will happen. A wise man lets the market alone when the averages disagree."

An easy way to gauge the direction of your investments is to watch the movement of interest rates. *Interest rates are the single most important factor in today's investment decisions.* You can forget about what you hear on the nightly news from Wall Street, what direction some money guru thinks the economy is headed, or the price of corn in Iowa. Interest rates and where they're headed are what the big money managers on Wall Street look at first. A change in interest rates can spark or dampen the stock market overnight.

If you approach the stock market the way an unsophisticated widow goes to a banker, trying to maximize her assets, remember that when interest rates fall the stock market will rise, since stocks generally go up when interest rates go down. When interest rates rise, the system works backwards, and the stock market usually falls.

When interest rates soar above 10% on insured savings accounts, move your assets into savings. You'll take advantage of money market rates that thrive on rising interest, and you'll also get out of the way of falling stock prices that higher interest rates could send into a tailspin. If interest rates fall, say to 8% or less on savings accounts and the stock market starts to take off, move back into the market. How much of your assets you commit to stock mutual funds and when you move in and out of savings is a decision that has to fit within your comfort zone.

Investors often get hurt because they are afraid to move in and out of the stock market. Part of their concern is the hefty commissions they've paid to get in and the commissions they'll have to pay to get out. That's why it's important to stay with no-load mutual funds. You can move freely in and out of the stock market as conditions change, taking advantage of a rising market or rising interest rates.

People tell me "I can't afford to sell some of my stocks. I can't afford to take the loss. I want to sit tight until I can sell and break even." The important point to remember when you invest in equities: You can never make money by sitting in the market and letting your losses run. That applies to both individual stocks you own and shares in a stock mutual fund.

Once you decide that it's time to invest in the stock market, it can be a tiresome chore picking the stock that's caught fire, or the one that, if you don't buy it, your broker feels you'll miss the investment opportunity of a lifetime.

Fortunately there's another way to invest in the market. That's by letting other people manage your money. Mutual funds allow you to spread your risks, move easily from fund to fund as your market strategy changes, and let you stay on top of your investments without staying up all night looking at the market charts and volume. Stock funds come in all varieties, depending on your investment objectives and tolerance for risks.

Stock funds can do everything for you except tell you when to buy and sell. Market conditions change so fast that I can't give you a solid, foolproof formula. It's a feel you have to develop for yourself.

That's why it's so important to understand that there is a time to be in stock mutual funds and a time to be out. If you pick a time when no one else wants to buy, you might be right. What's important, when you seek an inflation hedge in the market, is to understand fully why you are buying. The answer to that question could be more important than what you are buying.

You can invest in three basic stock funds: one for maximum capital gains that invests in stocks of small, fast-growing companies; one for long-term growth that buys stocks of companies with solid earnings and better-than-average potential for growth; and one that combines growth with income by concentrating on blue chips for capital gains and dividends. What you'll be looking for is which family of funds has consistently performed best over the long term. Consider too the number and types of funds within the family. A greater variety gives you more investment choices. For example, Boston's Fidelity Group has twenty-six funds, Philadelphia's Vanguard group has twenty-two funds.

For those new in the market, I'd put 75% of my stock-market money in conservative growth and income funds, 25% in long-term growth. Once you get the hang of it, you'd like to expand your risk, I'd reverse the ratio. If you want more risk by moving into smaller, faster growing companies, I'd put 50% of my money into maximum capital gains funds and 50% into long-term growth funds. What's important is that you stay within your comfort zone. Aggressive funds are likely to thrive in a roaring bull market—and crash just as fast. You may not have the stomach for sharp ups and downs. After all, how you make money is often as important to your well being as what you make.

OTHER INVESTMENTS. If you can tolerate a little more risk and if you're in a 40% or higher tax bracket, you might want to consider putting some of your equity money into a tax shelter. For $5,000 or $10,000 you can buy a piece of a $10 million high-rise office building or apartment complex. You'll get tax advantages and possibly income. But remember, as I said in chapter 7, these investments are not liquid—you're usually stuck with the deal for three to six years until the building is sold. You can also lose part or all of your investment. And your loss could even exceed the tax gain.

Before you plunge into any limited partnership, check out the track record of previous real estate deals before you invest. Try to get the names of people who have been in the partnership's previous real estate investments; find out how they feel about their current investment before you rush in with your cash.

Tax shelters are available from brokers, but most tax shelters are sold by financial planners. Good financial planners spend a great deal of time checking out the tax shelter deals and how they can fit into your overall financial plans. When you are tempted to buy a tax shelter, remember the age-old rule on speculative investments: Invest your time before you invest your money.

The investment strategy I've outlined is a balanced approach to making money in the eighties. It's what my letters and callers on my radio money programs tell me they want. It's a program that can fit your own personal struggle for saving and investing in the confusing financial marketplace we find ourselves in today. But, above all, any program you follow must be flexible and you must grasp the principles that will enable you to adapt your strategy to changing situations.

9

THE RETIREMENT YEARS:
DON'T TOUCH MY CAPITAL

Growing old in America is not always a trip through the gates of a retirement village with money in your pocket. Once you're retired, society no longer believes you're one hundred percent useful, and it hardly looks after you at all. Financial institutions, on the other hand, step up their drumbeat to attract your nest egg. Like psychologists, they try to discover your current attitude about saving, why you're more inclined to save than spend, why you put a premium on safety.

Most people today who face or are in retirement come from a lifetime of work in which they just got by financially. They remember few frills in a life that centered on paying for necessities. During their working years there were few places for savings—often they were limited to banks and savings and loans paying 3-5% simple interest.

Up until the early sixties financial management was translated into dealing with money problems day to day. The present retirees are the last generation to retire with thirty-year service pins and Social Security. The troubled economic times that shaped their working lives left little opportunity to enhance their career prospects by changing jobs. They equated long-term company employment with safety. Even when they retire financially well off they remain fearful of falling behind in their obligations. They often refuse to carry credit cards or incur any form of debt.

Once retired, in the confusing money times of the eighties, most people are preoccupied with holding on to what they have. Sometimes they hold so tightly that they lose more in purchasing power and taxes than they save in money. Change is a worrisome prospect, especially when it means changing a lifetime of saving habits. Clinging tightly to the safety of their bank passbook savings account paying 5¼% interest—earning at most a 4% after-tax return—they are reluctant to explore new ways to save with federal insurance protection plans offering almost twice the interest on their money. They are still living with the Great Depression.

The decision to retire is now up to each individual, Congress having done away with most mandatory retirement rules up to age seventy. But my letters and conversations with hundreds of people reaching society's acceptable retirement age tell me it's not always a dollars and cents decision. As you grow older you also need to change your attitude toward aging. Often people nearing retirement take in all the negative attitudes and apply them to themselves. Once retired, they believe they're not worth anything in our competitive, get-ahead society.

We're told to plan ahead so we'll know what income we'll need, what our living arrangements should be, and how we can maintain our good health. Yet, for most of us, thinking about old age is unpleasant work. Deborah Blagg, writing in the *Harvard Business School Bulletin* in 1981, believes, "It is a natural instinct to consider such issues as aging and retirement in abstract terms; we find it difficult to personalize issues pertaining to our own mortality. The critical faculties we use with great success in other areas of our lives are often very elusive when we attempt to bring them to bear on these issues."

Loren Dunton, in his book *The Vintage Years*, brings to life our feelings and our inner thoughts as we grow old. "As you grow older, a lot of physical problems or other difficulties that you encounter magnify themselves. When somebody invites you to dinner, or you go out to a restaurant, you are not impressed. In the first place, it's so dark, you can't read the menu. In the second place, you're stumbling all over because you can't pick your feet up. The food is laid down in front of you and it all looks the same and it's all running together. So you taste it, it tastes the same. The steak that the kids say tastes great, you say, 'Well, you're lucky you got a good piece, mine's tough.' Your dentures are popping up and down, and they don't really know what the hell's the matter with you. What's the whole point of aging? You wonder. These are the little insidious, normal, day-to-day things that face us when we're old."*

I'll never forget a program I did last year, "Are You Happy in Retirement?" Most of my guests and follow-up letters focused on changing your attitude in retirement. It's better, they told me, to retire early with the right attitude than to retire later with the wrong attitude. The reverse was also true, they said. It's better to retire late with the right attitude than to retire early with the wrong attitude. Ronald Reagan was a good example. Many felt that his attitude was shaped by his activity and his wealth, not his age.

The first suggestion was that if you don't want to work any longer, admit it. Just tell people you want to retire. What happens all too often with people who want to retire, especially if they feel defensive about it, is they make up some story about ill health or being displaced on the job. They gradually get tagged with those troubles, and worse, with the self-image of someone who is not up to the stress or savvy of retirement.

My guests who have succeeded in the transition from work to retirement believe you need to ask yourself several important questions before you make a decision to retire:

Will your income in retirement give you peace of mind? Not how much money you'll have or you can collect, but will you have piece of mind in your lifestyle after retirement? How much money people believe they need in retirement varies widely and rules to fit everyone are meaningless. Your first goal, if you retire, is to make sure you've allowed for your peace of mind.

Can you become active after you retire? Can you find new challenges and satisfactions to replace your active working life? This may be the most critical factor in your decision to retire. If your immediate transition is from active work to meaningless leisure you could be in trouble. Sixty-five-year-olds are not meant to run marathons one day and stand still the next. What's more, if you haven't found anything you enjoy doing by the time you reach your normal retirement age, you probably won't once you retire.

Many people who have been retired ahead of schedule by a harsh economy refuse to stay retired. They have begun second careers, typically more adventurous than those they left. As more and more

*Loren Dunton, *The Vintage Years,* Ten Speed Press, Berkeley, CA.

companies jettison their workers to stay afloat in these turbulent times, and as increasing numbers of workers break away from the 9-5 routine when they reach sixty-two and qualify for Social Security, second careers are rapidly on the rise. Many second careers offer a chance to fulfill a fantasy or vary life's pattern. Many early leavers seek the psychological rewards of work more than the money. At fifty-nine, an early retiree said he needed to head back to work. "After I retired, I sat home for three months. Now I'm going full out, one hundred percent on the job. I will never retire." In answer to my question, "When are you going to retire?" a spry man in his seventies told me he didn't plan on retiring. "If you like what you're doing why in hell retire?"

Have you decided where you'll live? This is a decision you need to make a year or two before you retire. You may want to move to another state and reduce your living expenses. Should you sell your present home, buy a new home or condo, or rent? These are tough decisions and you'll need the time to explore your options and make the necessary financial plans in advance.

When do you want to retire? The government has pushed mandatory retirement where you work up to age seventy. One of the interesting points that came out of the program on retirement was that many people decide to retire and then just retire, often at the earliest possible time with no thought as to when may be the best time to change their lifestyle, to prepare themselves for a new way of life.

One point about the timing of your transition from working to collecting benefits keeps recurring on my radio and television programs. I want to pass it on if you're concerned about your retirement security. Once you begin retirement and start to collect your benefits, there are few reverse gears. Most of us can't back up in time and start over.

Our nation's century-old retirement system is out of date. The entire structure continues to rest on the basic principles that husbands and wives will retire together, that women always marry and never divorce and never, but never, work outside the home. Social Security, designed on this principle, offers one-earner couples higher benefits than two-earner couples, even though both families have identical incomes, and in the latter case, both the husband and wife paid costly Social Security taxes throughout their working lives.

It would be naive for any of us to believe that historical and institutional retirement practices will miraculously disappear. They won't. With the mounting federal budget deficits staring it in the face, Congress will be reluctant to enact any major changes in a male-oriented pension system of the 1930s. Even a minor change in the way we retire could run into billions of dollars.

The prospects in retirement are not all doom and gloom. There is much that you can do to protect your future security. You'll need to make plans that few before you have ever made in order to battle inflation and taxes during your retirement. There can be little doubt that retirees' income will be hurt by inflation in the years to come. On the other hand, the more we seek a solution to the fear of dependence, the more inner freedom and strength we gain. It is when we assume responsibility for our own problems that our lives begin to make that vital shift from dependence to independence. If you now become realistic, well grounded in how to plan and protect your retirement security, and if you understand that, more than anything else, the system has now made you responsible for your own welfare, you can believe in yourself. For belief in self is the bottom line, and it belongs to all of us who have sprung free.

From listening to the problems people face in retirement, in talking with them about Social Security and pensions, and trying to understand a period of life I've yet to face, I've designed an overall money management plan. It's not going to work for everyone. No money plan can. But you can take the basic money management ideas and apply them to your individual situation when they fit. It's at least a road map in the direction you should be headed if you're going to stay ahead in the money game.

A Money Management Plan in Retirement

SOCIAL SECURITY. Substantial changes have been made over the years in the way Social Security pays out its benefits. The Social Security Act of 1935 marked a bold step toward financial security in retirement. Over the years the system has improved to a point where it now lifts millions of the elderly and disabled out of poverty and enables millions more to live their lives with dignity and basic comfort. Before Social Security the elderly and the disabled and their children were in desperate shape. Nine out of ten people over sixty-five had no pensions, public or private. These accomplishments must not be forgotten by the younger workers who are now being asked to pay ever-mounting payroll taxes to continue a system that will, in turn, help to support them in retirement. During this fifty-year span, we as a nation have moved from a point where society expected the elderly to take care of themselves—possibly with a little help from their families—to where most Americans now believe everyone has a *right* to security in retirement. What is becoming obvious, as Social Security continues to drown in an endless sea of red ink, is that the pendulum may have swung too far toward dependence on the system in retirement.

Nobody needs a weatherman to see which way the winds are blowing. Congress will be forced to boost taxes continually and cut back on the benefits to keep the massive retirement system from going under. Your first objective will be to learn how to collect the benefits.

COLLECTING SOCIAL SECURITY. You've been looking at your Social Security payroll taxes for years; now it's time to start collecting the benefits. You'll be competing with more than thirty-five million people already collecting benefits who flood local offices each day. And it will grow. Latest Census Bureau estimates give striking proof that the graying of America is in full stride. Almost 12% of America's population is now sixty-five or older, a record. That's almost double the percentage of older Americans in 1940. The second fastest growing group? People 85 and older.

You can avoid some of the most common pitfalls during your first year of collecting benefits by recognizing from the start that you will be dealing with an overworked and paper-snarled bureaucracy basically controlled by one giant computer—which periodically seems to come unplugged. Social Security regulations—which, through successive congressional changes, read like new car warranties written in Greek—can easily result in frustrating hours spent in the local office or wasted days trying to get information you could obtain with a simple postcard or telephone call. Here's how to attack the system in earnest:

Tip One. At least six months before you plan to retire take the necessary documentation, in person, to the local office. Be sure to take the following papers on your first visit

- Your Social Security card and that of your spouse if you are both going to draw benefits.

192

- Proof of age for both you and your spouse.
- Marriage certificate or copy thereof.
- The most recent W-2 tax withholding form from your job.
- Birth certificates of any children for whom you want to claim benefits.

Tip Two. Use the telephone. It beats standing in line, and a surprising amount of contact with the local office can be made over the phone. In many cases you'll find out what documents you will need once you get to the office.

Tip Three. Stay away from the local office on Monday, the busiest day of the week. Also avoid the third or fourth of each month when retirees who failed to receive their checks will descend on the office en masse to register complaints.

Tip Four. Don't shop around for higher benefits. Everyone's benefits are set by law. You can double-check your benefits by mailing a special post card, available at any Social Security office and from most financial planners, with your Social Security number, your date of birth and your address. You must sign the card to get this confidential information. Be sure to write "include retirement benefit estimate" along the bottom of the card.

Tip Five. If you are collecting benefits on the basis of another person's earning record, such as that of a spouse, your Social Security number will be different from your claim number. If you use your own number and not that of the person who is collecting the benefits, you'll come up empty handed. To find your account you must use the Social Security number of the person on whose earnings your benefits are based.

Tip Six. Once you have filed your claim you should receive your check by the third of the month. If your check fails to find your mailbox, and you begin to panic, call the local office and file a lost claim report. Computer malfunction or not, usually the longer you wait to trace your own money, the longer you will have to wait for your check.

The Last Tip. See if you can talk with someone who has just been through the process of successfully filing and collecting Social Security benefits. Claim procedures frequently change. This up-to-date information could be very helpful.

When you begin to collect your benefits will affect your monthly income for the rest of your life. Like all retirement plans there are no reverse gears. The maximum benefit currently available at age sixty-five is $709 a month. With a dependent spouse, also age sixty-five, the benefit is increased 50%, to $1,063. Social Security's *average* benefit for those retiring at age sixty-five, however, is about $420 a month, and with a dependent spouse, about $630. If the worker is sixty-five but the dependent spouse is younger, which is the typical case, the wife's benefit is reduced accordingly.

If you decide to retire at age sixty-two, your expected benefits at age sixty-five are reduced by 20%. For every month you continue to work before you begin to draw your Social Security benefits between the ages of sixty-two and sixty-five, your expected benefit is increased on the basis of 6⅔% a year. One of Social Security's major cash drains is that millions of Americans simply cannot wait to break out of the job market. They have discovered that by taking 80% of their benefits at age sixty-two, they can draw three years of benefit checks before they reach sixty-five. That could amount to over $30,000 of tax-free income! At sixty-five a retiree with a dependent spouse would need at least twelve years simply to catch up.

As late as 1956 only 13% of American workers retired "early," or before the normal Social Security age of sixty-five. Today the number of early quitters is over 70% and rising fast. That's why there's talk in Congress of extending the age for regular benefits up to sixty-eight, with early retirement beginning at age sixty-four.

If you retire and continue to work, you can lose $1 of benefits for each $2 you earn from salary or self-employed income when your work income exceeds around $7,000 if you are sixty-five or older, around $5,000 between the ages of sixty-two and sixty-five. The amount you can earn without losing benefits goes up each year, depending on wages and inflation. If you're past age seventy-two, you won't lose Social Security benefits regardless of your earnings. If you're in doubt, check for the current amount with your local office.

TAXING SOCIAL SECURITY BENEFITS. If you are retired or are looking down the road toward retirement, you probably breathed more easily when Congress "rescued" Social Security. One of the ways to keep the system from running out of cash is to tax part of the benefits we receive. But many people—particularly higher-income couples—will catch their breath when they realize how heavily the taxing of benefits will affect them. The new rules take effect in 1984 and you'll need to add up three things: your adjusted gross income, interest income from tax-free bonds, and one-half of your Social Security benefits. If the total is more than $25,000 for a single person or $32,000 for married couples, you'll pay the new benefit tax on the lesser of either one-half of the benefits received, or one-half the excess of the total over the base amount.

For example: a retired couple who received Social Security benefits of $12,000 in 1984, $15,000 from a company pension, and $15,000 in other income would have some taxes to pay. Adding their pensions and other income ($30,000) and one-half their Social Security benefits ($6,000) gives a total of $36,000, which is $4,000 more than the base amount for a married couple. They would be taxed on half the excess, or on $2,000. Regardless of your total income, you can never be taxed on more than 50% of the Social Security benefits you receive. Taxes will not come out of your monthly Social Security checks; that would be a nightmare even Congress wants to duck. You'll pay your taxes when you file your income tax returns each year.

There's an interesting sidelight to Social Security's tax-free benefits. In the early days of the program, in an attempt to get around the double tax deduction on the same money, the Treasury Department ruled that funds received in retirement were a "gratuity." But in looking for ways to give Social Security a cash transfusion while encouraging older workers to postpone retirement, Congress has hit on the idea of taxing benefits. The rationale for taxing to the grave is this. When your employer pays half your Social Security taxes he takes a tax deduction. The worker pays no tax on these employer contributions. When the retiree receives Social Security benefits only half of the contributions to support these payments have been taxed. That's why the law says that you can only be taxed on Social Security benefits up to 50% of the money you receive. That, according to the IRS, is the part that escaped taxation when the contributions were paid by your employer. Any future financial planning you do with Social Security should be based on an increasing percent of your benefit becoming taxable, up to half of the money you receive.

How Much Can I Count on Social Security?

The real value of any retirement plan is the percentage, or *replacement ratio,* of your final salary you can collect in retirement. For example, if your salary before retirement was $25,000 and your retirement benefits were $6,250, then your replacement ratio is 25%.

What you're not being told, as Social Security continues to surprise retirees, is that the replacement ratio for Social Security has been going down and down. I'd feel a lot more comfortable if Social Security would tell us less about the changes in taxes and benefits and more about just how much we can expect when we retire.

In fact, one big way to keep its financial house from collapsing is to let Social Security continue to reduce the percentage of final salary we can collect at retirement. To put that in perspective, the law now on the books will reduce Social Security's replacement ratio for "average income workers"—about $15,000 in 1982—from 46.6% in 1979 to 42.0% in 1982, to 36.6% in 1987. For those with Social Security's "maximum income"—about $32,700 in 1982— the replacement ratio will be reduced from 34.8% in 1979 to 24.9% in 1982, to 21.8% in 1987.

In the lingo of retirement income, Social Security will continue to provide less and less of our preretirement salary in retirement.

MEDICARE. Before you retire you are probably covered by a group medical plan where you work. You will be offered the "right" to convert this group policy into an individual policy, usually within 30 days after you leave the company. Unless you or your spouse are already ill or you expect to collect benefits from the policy it's usually not a good idea to convert the group medical insurance to your name and pay the premiums. That's because the insurance company already knows only people with major illnesses will convert their former group policy and they have substantially reduced the benefits and hiked the premiums.

Your best bet is to sign up for Medicare at your Social Security office three months before you reach age sixty-five. Medicare is made up of two parts. *Part A* helps you pay the costs when you are in the hospital and is free once you reach sixty-five, whether or not you retire.

Once in the hospital, you'll face a $304 deductible for that illness. Then for the first sixty days Medicare will pay the rest of the bills. For the next thirty days you pay $76 a day, the next sixty days, $152 a day. If you are out of the hospital for sixty days, you can start the program over again. The good news is that, according to Social Security, 95% of the people over sixty-five are out of the hospital in less than fifteen days.

Part B is voluntary supplemental coverage for nonhospital expenses and has a current monthly premium of $12.20. *Part B* is based on a calendar year and you must pay the first $75 of expenses and then Medicare will pick up 80% of the *allowable* charges.

Social Security says that 80% of the allowable charges now pays for about 67% of the actual charges. *Part B* does not cover many important items, such as drugs, hearing aids, dental expenses, or eyeglasses.

If you or someone you know does not qualify for Social Security benefits, they can buy *Part A* for $113 a month and *Part B* for $12.20 a month, a reflection of just how expensive medicare insurance has become.

PRIVATE MEDICAL INSURANCE. To pay for the medical expenses not picked up by Medicare, you can buy a Medicare Supplement policy. These policies help you pay for the hospital charges over sixty days and part of the regular medical expenses Medicare does not pick up under *Part B*. When you look for this coverage stay with the big names, Blue Cross, Blue Shield, Mutual of Omaha, Prudential.

The premium should be about $385 to $400 a year for ages sixty-five to sixty-nine, and $475 to $500 for ages seventy to seventy-four for the minimum coverage. If you can afford better coverage—paying a greater percentage of the medical bills Medicare does not pay—the annual premiums should be about $600 to $650 for ages 65 to 69 and $750 to $800 for ages seventy to seventy-four. Like most private insurance plans, you'll have a six month exclusion for illness under treatment when you sign up for the policy. After six months, all medical expenses under the policy will be covered.

RETIREMENT PLANS. One of your first priorities should be to check and see if you have kept records of vested retirement benefits in your previous jobs. These are the assets in your previous employers' retirement plans that are held in your name until you retire. When you write to your previous employers, be sure to ask for the latest copy of the plan's *Summary Plans Description Booklet*. This booklet is available free and your employer is required by law to see that you receive a copy if you ask. It should explain, in common English, how the plan works and how you can begin drawing your benefits.

What you'll need to look for prior to retirement is the type of plan your employer has provided during your working years. If you were covered under a *pension* you were promised certain monthly benefits based on your income and years of service. Your pension is insured by the government's Pension Benefit Guaranty Corporation, which takes over defined-benefit plans that terminate without enough assets to continue to pay the promised benefits.

If you were covered by a *money purchase pension* plan, your employer has only promised to contribute a certain percentage of your salary each year, not to provide a pre-set benefit when you retire. Your retirement benefit will be, as the name of the plan indicates, whatever the money in your account will purchase at the time of your retirement. Federal insurance is not available for these plans.

If you were covered by a *profit sharing* plan, contributions to the plan will have been made only when the employer had a profit and in amounts the company decided it could spare from year to year. Again, federal insurance is not available for profit sharing plans.

Often it is best to ask for a lump-sum distribution of the assets held on your behalf before you agree to take the monthly payments. If you receive a lump-sum distribution, consider rolling over the money into an IRA. That way you can withdraw the money as you need the cash and the balance will continue to earn tax-deferred interest income.

If you are offered fixed pension benefits, be sure to plan in advance how you will take the money. You have a choice of an income for the life of the worker or a joint pension arrangement which pays an income for the life of either the worker or spouse. Most pension plans work like this: If a worker elects to receive the pension only so long as he lives—let's say the benefit works out to $850 a month—then all benefits stop upon his death. If the worker elects joint benefits—called survivor benefits—then his monthly benefit might be reduced to, say $700 a month. He will receive this pension as long as he lives, but in the event he dies first, his widow could continue to receive his pension benefits under the joint benefit arrangement. The actual benefit will depend on the widow's age at the time of her husband's death and the terms of the retirement plan, but the benefits will be reduced to less than the $700 the husband formerly received.

If you are married and if a survivor benefit from the company's retirement plan is important to your long-range financial planning, don't let the often confusing and complex pension rules stand in your way. Make sure you and/or your spouse have made an election on the payment of benefits prior to retirement. If the husband, for example, retires and begins to collect the larger sum based on his lifetime only, *it's too late to back up and start over.* His monthly pension benefit will automatically stop at his death.

On IRAs, I suggest that you keep the money you have accumulated in your IRA working and earning tax-deferred income as long as you can. It makes good sense to use other savings outside your IRA first. These assets earn taxable income, slashing your net savings at a time when you need the maximum earning power. You must begin withdrawing IRA money when you reach age seventy and a half, and the distributions must be taken in amounts that exhaust the account by the actuarially predicted year of your death. HOUSING. Another major decision when you retire is where to live. In small towns and cities, people tend to stay put. They are no longer worried about not being able to have the things they once expected. After retirement their lifestyle remains basically on track. Their social activities continue uninterrupted and they tend to spend more time with their children and friends. For many people, it's important to keep life-disrupting changes to a minimum, to keep a positive attitude as they position themselves in retirement.

In large cities, where many people already live in apartments or condos, the trend is to pack up and move to a retirement village. Where to live is often not a dollars-and-cents decision. The best place to live is where you and your family are happy. And happiness doesn't come from the home itself; it comes from where the home is located.

If you've decided to move, consider renting a furnished apartment for a month or two in the area and act as if you permanently lived there. You can go shopping, read the newspapers, talk to the people—they'll tell you what they know about the living conditions. After all, you've got plenty of time and you don't want to move again in a short time. You want to settle in.

If you retire with a limited monthly income and if your home is paid for, you might consider selling it and renting. It's an emotional trauma few of us want to face, but it could make good financial sense if you need to improve your basic standard of living. By letting your major money machine work for you in retirement you can take advantage of the law's provisions on the one-time sale of your home which lets you escape taxes on the profits up to $125,000. If you save this amount in a federally insured savings account, for example, based on today's interest rates you could receive an income of about $950 a month for life. (The amount will follow the current interest rates, and could rise or fall in the years to come. The hope is that if inflation reignites so will interest rates and your income will rise to meet the higher costs.) If your rent is, say, $350 a month, that's $600 a month extra income to help provide the comfort and dignity that's so important in retirement.

Congress is also working on a plan whereby retirees could sell their residences to financial institutions—something like buying a home in reverse—and continue to live in them while collecting annuity income from the sale of the home. The new law would give the retirees' the right to take the homeowners' tax exclusion on profits from the sale and let the financial institution depreciate the property even though the sellers continue to live in it. Both the Canadians and British are way ahead of us in the use of residences to finance retirement income. In England, it's called a *home income plan*. The plan provides an immediate increase in income for life, with the security of continued home occupancy.

I don't recommend that you sell your home unless or until you need the money to maintain a decent living standard or unless you plan to buy a new one in another location.

WILLS. A lot of smart people don't have wills. They can't find the time to sit down and make the decisions that someone else will have to make after they're gone. Having a will is the only way you can distribute your assets according to your wishes. Federal estate taxes have been slashed upon the death of the first spouse to die, but it's not taxes that should give you concern. You should consider a trustee, usually a bank or other third party corporation that lives forever, to administer your estate. The trustee can care financially for your dependents and carry out your wishes as expressed in your will.

If you want to stay ahead in the money game you should spend the few dollars it takes to meet with an attorney and explore what steps you need to take to save taxes and provide for your loved ones. Most of you won't take this advice. Few people have an up-to-date will. But I ask you to do it nevertheless. The most important thing money can buy as we get older is peace of mind—and a good feeling about the future.

A Financial Plan

SAVING MONEY. Once we are retired we become concerned for the safety of our money. As one guest on my program put it, "Now I have maintenance worries, not growth worries." With no new money in the future, we remain fearful of falling behind on our obligations. We often keep large amounts of money in an insured savings account, not for the interest we can earn, but for the safety of our money.

Books are rarely written about how we feel about money. But over and over again people tell me that in retirement their primary goal in life is to remain safe. They often spend so much time and effort in not losing, they rarely think in terms of winning. Since safety is their prime concern, they often disrupt their lifestyle and the enjoyment retirement should bring in the belief that their problems can be solved by more money.

In this era of financial deregulation and a threatened return of increasing inflation, money management will become more important than the mere act of saving. The individual who continues to lock up all his money in fixed-rate savings, the self-denier, the compulsive bargain hunter will do less well than the individual who strikes out in pursuit of higher earnings with adequate safety and one eye out for the tax man. I'm not suggesting that you take risks that will keep you awake at night. You need an overall strategy to increase your assets and your peace of mind, not jeopardize them. This is the hardest advice to follow because most of us continue to believe locking up our money in a passbook account will make us safe.

What financial advice I give is based on the mathematical equation, not on the human equation. That's because I don't know you, how you feel about money, how you feel about the possibility of becoming dependent upon others. People often ask me about financial problems when I know they want me to tell them to follow their heart, not their pocketbook. And that's all right. Peace of mind can often bring more happiness than the extra dollars they might make.

If you are willing to explore some new ways to save your money—with the safety I think you need—here are some places you might look.

CREDIT UNION. Consider staying with your credit union, if you belong to one prior to retirement, or joining one when you retire. Credit unions were formed to help employees save and borrow money during their working lives. But credit unions have been expanded to include residents of entire communities and your local area may have just such a plan. If not, check out the blood relation features that allow you to join if any of your relatives now belong. The list may include your in-laws, your cousins—almost anyone you can connect by blood or marriage.

Credit unions offer the same federal insurance protection as savings & loans and banks. The National Credit Union Administration [NCUA], like the FDIC and the FSLIC will protect your savings up to $100,000 for each account. They usually offer three types of savings accounts. Passbook savings for amounts of less than $5,000 earn about the same as other insured saving accounts pay. One-year term Share Certificate accounts on amounts of $5,000 up to $10,000 usually earn more than insured savings at banks and thrifts. Share Certificates of over $10,000 can often earn as much as 1-1½% more. Credit unions are not under the same rules and regulations as banks and thrifts; they have more flexibility in setting their interest rates and savings plans.

T-BILLS. Another safe place to expand your money management, get the feel of moving out of locked-up savings plans, is in T-bills. Covered in the previous chapter, they can often pay a higher rate than insured savings and you can buy them from your broker, banker, or by mail. They provide an added bonus: you pay no state income tax on your interest income.

SAVING WITH LIMITED RISKS. If you are scared to death about the prospect of no longer living from paycheck to paycheck, you need very little of my advice. You can continue to put your money into savings at a bank or thrift and pay your taxes on the interest income. As long as the interest rate you earn after taxes remains above the inflation rate you can keep your head above water. As long as you don't need to withdraw your capital and you can live on the interest income, you can sit tight. Tax savings and higher interest rates will not tempt you out of your insured savings account, and that's all right.

Most retired Americans fall into this group. It's the typical way to retire from a life of hard work and preplanned savings. It's also the way our government has set for us to handle money in retirement. Because tax saving opportunities are tightly linked to earned income, those in retirement often find few ways to defer income. Since federal insurance is tightly locked around the insured savings accounts, retirees are often too scared to go elsewhere. In fact, it takes a great deal of courage to break away from the government's long-established way to hold money in retirement.

If you feel you have the courage to take limited risks, or if you face a tax problem, you might want to consider the following savings opportunities that have sprung up in this new era of financial deregulation.

MONEY MARKET FUNDS INVESTED IN GOVERNMENT SECURITIES. This is a good place to hold short-term money, much like a regular money market mutual fund. Your money is safe, and as in all mutual funds, professional money managers will devote their full time to keeping up with the changes in the financial marketplace. A good way to look over this money market fund is to pick up a prospectus from Sears in their Dean Witter Financial Network. Called the Sears U.S. Government Money-Market Trust, it's a no-load mutual fund that invests only in U.S. government securities and securities from government agencies.

UNIT INVESTMENT TRUSTS. If you need maximum income, you might consider investing part of your cash into Government Securities Income Funds invested in Ginnie Maes (Government National Mortgages). These trusts, and the risks associated with them, were covered in chapter 3. They allow you to go into a bond fund made up of government-backed mortgages that pay as much as 2 or 3% more than insured savings accounts. Again, the income you receive from these trusts will include part of your capital, which is returned as the bonds are paid off, and your interest income. If you wish to keep your money working, have your returned capital (and interest, if you like) automatically reinvested in the trust.

If income taxes are a consideration, consider the new Unit Investment Trusts invested in municipal tax-free bonds. Some are protected by FSLIC insurance, but your safety can lie with the brokerage firm that offers the tax-free bond trust. Big names like Merrill Lynch, Dean Witter, Prudential-Bache, and Shearson/American Express should give you the comfort you need to place part of your cash into these trusts.

Interest rates in these new tax-free trusts are now running about 1% higher than insured savings accounts, and after taxes in a modest 30% bracket, that's a big difference in your net savings. If insured savings are paying 8%, the equivalent taxable rate for these tax-free trusts is about 12%. If you invest in a Municipal Investment Trust or tax-free mutual fund within your state, you can grab double tax-free income—you pay no federal or state income tax on your interest income—and put a lot more money right where it belongs. In your pocket.

Tax-free bonds, offered by a broker, a mutual fund, or by your savings and loan or bank are about as conservative an opportunity as you can find to get so high a return. They're not without some risks, but you can stay on top of your investment by watching interest rates and keep the risks to a minimum. (Remember, if interest rates rise after you buy your bonds, the value of your investment, should you want to sell, could decline and you'd be earning less than market rates; if interest rates fall after you buy your bonds, the value of your investment could rise and you'd be earning more than market interest rates.)

STOCK MARKET—AND OTHER INVESTMENTS THAT GO UP AND DOWN. "I'm retired," the matronly voice echoed through the broker's office. As she entered the manager's office, her eyes afire with panic, she said, "I bought Fireworks United stock at $20 a couple of weeks ago and now it's dropped to $16. At my age I can't afford to lose money in the market."

"Why did you buy it in the first place?" the manager asked.

"Well, it was going up and up and besides I think it's in the same business as Bigtime Explosion which made my son a lot of money. I didn't buy Bigtime because at $50 a share the stock costs more than I wanted to spend. You know," she said, looking into the manager's face for a sign of understanding, "I really can't afford to lose my money."

The plight of this retired investor is indicative of today's stock market. Too many unknowledgeable risk takers are playing the game in a market that seems to be rising and falling every day, making and at the same time losing money for those who rush into the Wall Street money game. Everyone wants to be an investment whiz. With the stock market moving to record levels on the Dow Jones, many older people have decided that money market funds or banks and savings and loans are terribly dull places to keep money. Besides the stock market, many older retired people are rushing into gold coins, collectibles, real estate deals—all at a time when inflation has cooled and the investment market may be in for a serious correction.

I'd feel a lot more comfortable if the recession were over and the recovery in full swing with a stable investment market before I went into the risk-taking business as a retiree. And, in retirement you can afford to wait until a time when almost no one else wants to buy. If conservative stock mutual funds are within your comfort zone, you can wait until the stock market has finished a major correction and the speculators have been forced to cash in their stock and retreat to the sidelines. Then you can put some of your cash in solid growth companies and ride the market back up. I'd begin to take profits as the market moves up to where I've made a 20 to 30% gain and put the money back into savings. I'd get out of the market altogether when my stock falls more than 15% off the record high for the stock. I may miss that last few upticks, but at least I can sleep at night.

Retiring successfully and happily is not easy. If I've learned anything, I'd say the most important single task you face is developing a positive attitude about yourself and your ability to learn what you need to know to manage your money. Your attitudes on savings can undergo a metamorphosis that will allow you to reach out and grab the higher earnings without the fear of losing all. I hope in some small way I've opened the door, helped you to find your pension benefits, delayed some taxes, and made your retirement years more secure.

I hope you'll continue to invest and save your money in ways that make you happy. It's your life, and your retirement years should be all that you can make them.

APPENDICES

Glossary of Economic and Investment Terms
Here are some definitions of many of the terms used in the book, plus other terms you might come across when you look into saving and investment money, planning your retirement income or seek tax-deferred or tax-free ways to accumulate money.

My definition isn't authoritative; its purpose is to make the idea more intelligible to someone who is not familiar with economic and investment terms. In most cases, I've defined a word in the way it's generally understood in saving and investment worlds, or as I've used it in the text.

ANNUITY: A contract with an insurance company that promises to pay fixed amounts periodically (monthly, yearly, etc.) over a given period of time or for life. You can buy an annuity with a single payment or with periodic payments over several years.

ANNUITY, TAX-DEFERRED: A contract with an insurance company on the same basis as a regular annuity, except the investments to build the annuity accumulate tax-deferred until the money is taken out. The income is then taxable as received. Congress recently changed the laws so that withdrawals are assumed to be interest income and taxable, and you can pay a 5% penalty if you withdraw the money before age 59½ and within the first ten years of the date of the annuity.

ASK PRICE: The price at which a broker/dealer offers to sell unlisted stock, other investment products.

BACK-END SALES CHARGE: A sales charge or sales commission that is paid when the investment is sold. Without an up-front sales charge, you pay a hefty sales commission on the total amount of your withdrawal, including not only your investments but all the interest or profits earned prior to withdrawal.

BANKER'S ACCEPTANCE: A postdated business check, usually for $50,000 or more, that has been "accepted" or guaranteed by the bank seeking your money as an investor.

BEAR MARKET: A period, usually on the stock exchanges, where the price trend is down.

BID PRICE: The price at which a broker/dealer will pay to buy an unlisted stock, or other investment products.

BIG BOARD: Another name for the New York Stock Exchange.

BLUE CHIP: A name for a nationally known company with wide acceptance of its products or services, and for its ability to pay its stockholders a regular dividend.

BREAK IN SERVICE: A pension plan that requires the employee to work continuously for a certain number of years to collect a pension at retirement. A break in service can occur when the employee is fired, laid off, or quits and returns to the company.

BROKER: An agent, often a stockbroker, who buys and sells securities, commodities, or other property on commission.

BULL MARKET: A period during which good news pushes the price trend up.

CAFETERIA FRINGE-BENEFIT PLANS: Where you put pre-tax wages into a "reimbursement account." The money never shows up on your W-2 form, and you can withdraw the money tax-free to pay for fringe-benefit-linked expenses such as legal advice, the kid's orthodontic work, care of an elderly parent, home/auto insurance—even a live-in housekeeper.

CALL OPTION: A right to purchase a specified investment at a fixed price on a specified date, or in most cases, prior to the specified date.

CALL PRIVILEGE: The right of a bond issuer (a company, city, or state that issued the bond) to repay the bond prior to its maturity date. This can happen when interest rates fall, because the bond issuer can call the old bond and issue a new one at a lower interest rate.

CAPITAL: The money paid into a company by its shareholders. It can also refer to the net assets of a person or a firm.

CAPITAL GAINS TAX: A way the IRS taxes profits made on the sale of investments. If you hold investments for one year or less—short-term gains—your capital gains are taxed as ordinary income, based on your personal tax rate. If you hold the investment for more than one year—a long-term gain—the maximum income tax rate is only 20%, and many times a great deal less.

CASH-VALUE LIFE INSURANCE: Life insurance that, in addition to paying benefits in the event of death, acts as a saving plan to keep the premiums level during your lifetime. The owner can borrow against the cash values in the policy during his lifetime by paying the insurance company the annual interest rate established in the policy. If a loan is outstanding at the time of death, the face amount of the policy will be reduced by the amount of the cash-value loan before payment is made to the beneficiary.

CD: Certificate of deposit. A deposit (or short-term savings account) represented by a certificate, usually from a bank, that is transferable.

CLOSED-END INVESTMENT COMPANY: An investment company, often a mutual fund, that issues a fixed number of shares.

COLLATERAL: An asset that is pledged for a loan, to be forfeited if repayment is not made.

COMMISSION: The broker's fee for buying or selling securities, or as an agent for property.

COMMON STOCK FUND: A mutual fund that invests all or most of its assets in common stocks.

COMPOUND INTEREST: Where interest is allowed to accumulate and earn additional interest on the retained interest income.

COMPOUND TAX-DEFERRED INTEREST: The magic of all retirement plans. Where interest is allowed to accumulate tax-free and the full amount of the interest is put to work to earn more interest income.

CONTRIBUTORY IRA: An IRA in which you make regular contributions from your paycheck each year.

COUPON RATE: The annual rate of interest, as a percentage of the face value, paid by a bond.

CUSTODIAN: An agent that keeps investments. All IRAs and

Keogh plans require a custodian to maintain assets and make reports of changes in the account.

DEALER: An individual or firm in the securities business acting as a principal rather than as an agent. A dealer buys for his own account and sells to a customer from his own inventory. Unlisted over-the-counter stocks are often bought and sold by a dealer.

DEFINED-BENEFIT PLAN: This is the correct name for a pension plan. A pension specifies the size of the benefit (usually in relation to your last working salary) and when the benefit can be paid. The cost of the plan is paid entirely by the employer.

DEFINED-CONTRIBUTION PLAN: This is the correct name for a money-purchase pension plan. The cost is paid by the employer. However, the benefits you receive will be only as much as the money in your account will buy when you retire. The employer is only required to make a contribution, not to provide a certain guaranteed benefit at retirement.

DEFLATION: The opposite of inflation. Deflation usually causes a fall in the general price levels.

DEMAND DEPOSIT: Bank deposits that can be withdrawn without penalty at any time, like a passbook savings account.

DEPENDENT STATUS: That part of the pension law that refers to benefits for dependent members of the family. Usually, retirement benefits—private or Social Security—are not available to dependents until the worker who earned the benefits has retired. This also applies to divorced women, who may be entitled to Social Security benefits based on their ex-husband's income, but who must wait until he retires to collect.

DEPOSIT ACCOUNT: A bank account with withdrawal restrictions. Also called a "time" deposit, because you agree to lock up your money for a set period of time.

DISCOUNT BOND: A bond that is selling, or was issued, at a dollar price below the par value. When interest rates rise after a bond is issued, the bond can trade at a discount since its current yield is now below the market rate of interest.

DISCOUNT BROKER: A broker who only buys and sells stocks and bonds. Without offering advice, making a market, or helping customers to buy and sell, discount brokers have cut commissions by as much as 75%. Most of the new discount brokers are springing up in banks and savings and loans.

DISCOUNT RATE: The interest rate charged by the Federal Reserve Bank on loans to commercial banks.

DISCRETIONARY ACCOUNT: An account that empowers a bank, broker, or financial adviser to make investment decisions on your behalf.

DIVIDEND: A payment by the corporation to its shareholders, like interest earned on a savings account. The dividend can vary with the corporation's profits and the amount of cash on hand.

DOLLAR-COST AVERAGING: A method of buying the same security at regular intervals with a fixed dollar amount. The idea is to buy when the price is low and high, to make purchases in good times and bad, to average out the price of the stock.

DOW JONES AVERAGES: The stock averages you see in the newspaper. There are three Dow Jones averages: The transportation, the utility, and the industrial stock averages. The most widely quoted is the industrial stock average.

EARNED INCOME: For tax purposes, income from wages, salary, or self-employment. Earned income is the only source you have to make contributions into IRAs and Keogh plans.

ECONOMIC RECOVERY TAX ACT OF 1981: This law gave us across-the-board income tax cuts, reduced long-term capital gains taxes, made headway against eliminating the marriage tax penalty by offering a working spouse deduction, and made a substantial reduction in estate and gift taxes. This is also the law that gave us the new expanded IRA and Keogh plans. Not only is every worker eligible to open an IRA, but maximum contributions were boosted to $2,000, and with a spousal IRA, up to $2,250.

EQUITY INVESTMENT: An investment in stock in which you are at risk if the value of the company goes down. Often equity investments in smaller firms do not pay a specific return to the investor.

ERISA: The Employee Retirement Income Security Act of 1974. This law cleaned up private pension abuse, provided pension plan insurance through the Pension Benefit Guaranty Corporation (PBGC), and gave us IRAs for employees who were not covered by a retirement plan where they worked.

EX-DIVIDEND: Meaning without dividend. The buyer of a stock selling ex-dividend does not receive the recently declared dividend. When stocks go ex-dividend, the stock tables include the symbol X following the name.

FEDERAL RESERVE SYSTEM: The central bank, made up of twelve Federal Reserve Banks, supervised by a Board of Governors who operate outside the control of Congress and the President. The current Chairman is Paul Volker.

GENERAL OBLIGATION BONDS: These municipal bonds are sold to finance public improvements and they are repaid by taxes. These projects include streets, water systems, schools, and police and fire stations.

GINNIE MAE: Mortgage-backed securities of the Government National Mortgage Association (GNMA). The government's way of providing money to the mortgage-lending institutions as a way of bringing investment funds into the real estate market.

GREAT AMERICAN MYTH: The idea on which our nation's retirement system is built: The traditional family—wage-earning dad, stay-at-home mom, two kids. Today, such families account for only 7% of all American households.

GROWTH FUND: A mutual fund whose rate of growth over a period of time is greater than that of the market in general.

INCOME FUND: A mutual fund with a primary objective of current income.

INFLATION: It's not an increase in prices, although prices do increase. It's a decrease in the value of your money, so that every dollar buys less.

INTEREST RATE: The interest paid annually, expressed as a percentage of $1,000 invested. For a bond this is the coupon rate.

ISSUER: The state, municipality, corporation, or whoever is selling the bonds.

JOINT AND SURVIVOR ANNUITY: A contract, usually with a insurance company, that promises to pay a regular sum to the annuitant for his or her life and then to continue the payments for the life of the surviving spouse.

KEOGH PLAN: Like an IRA, but available only to self-employed individuals. (Also called an HR-10.) If you are self-employed, you can contribute as much as $30,000 in a Keogh plan *and* then make the maximum contribution into your IRA!

LESS-THAN-ROUND LOT: A stock transaction that incurs special charges (less than 100 shares) and possible delays in executing your order to buy or sell. See ODD LOT.

LEVERAGE: Any arrangement in which you can control a large sum of money with a small down payment.

LIABILITIES: All debts and claims against a company. When liabilities exceed assets the company is insolvent.

LIMITED PARTNERSHIP: A partnership in which investors are limited partners with a limited liability for the partnership's obligations.

LIQUIDITY: You are said to have liquidity with your savings and investments if you can turn the assets into cash quickly.

LISTED STOCK: The stock of a company traded on a securities exchange.

MANAGEMENT FEE: The fee paid to the investment manager of a mutual fund. The fee, usually about one-half of one percent up to three-quarters of one percent of the average net assets annually, is paid by the mutual fund shareholders. This is not the same as the sales charge, which is paid at the time of purchase.

MARGIN: The amount paid to buy stocks on margin. The balance of the purchase price is on credit at prevailing interest rates.

MARKET ORDER: The order you give a broker to buy or sell securities at the best price then available.

MARKETABILITY: This means that you can sell your investment at the market rate, whenever you wish. When you invest, be sure to check the marketability of your investment so that if your needs change or your investment goes sour you can sell quickly and easily at the market rate.

MATURITY: A date on which a contractual obligation is due, such as the repayment of a bond.

MONEY MARKET ACCOUNT: A savings account at a bank or S&L that pays current interest on your savings.

MONEY MARKET CHECKING: A checking account that pays you interest on the money that remains in your account. Currently the minimum balance is $2,500, and if your account balance slides below that figure your interest falls to the passbook rate, or 5.25%.

MONEY MARKET FUND: A mutual fund that invests only money market instruments and pays the current interest earned on these investments.

MUNICIPAL BOND: A bond issued by a state, county, city government, or by a public agency. Income from municipal bonds is free of federal income tax.

MUTUAL FUND: A fund that invests in stocks, bonds, or other securities. The fund assumes the obligation to redeem its shares at the net asset value of the fund upon request.

NASD: The National Association of Securities Dealers. An association of brokers and dealers in the over-the-counter securities market. The NASD is the watchdog of the industry with the powers to expel members and enforce rules of fair practice for the public good.

NASDAQ: The name given the automated information network that gives brokers and dealers price quotations on securities traded over-the-counter.

NYSE: An acronym for the New York Stock Exchange, the nation's leading stock exchange.

ODD LOT: An amount of stock less than the established 100-share unit of trading. On an odd-lot market order, the price is based on the first round-lot transaction that occurs on the stock exchange floor following receipt of the odd-lot order. The extra charge for odd-lot trading over round-lot trading is about 12.5 cents a share.

OPTION: The right to buy or sell specific securities or properties at a specified price within a specified time.

ORDINARY INCOME: For tax purposes, income from all sources except capital gains.

OVER-THE-COUNTER MARKET: A market that trades in unlisted securities, conducted by broker/dealers through negotiation rather than through the use of an auction system as in the stock exchanges. The quotes are offered as bid and asked.

PAR VALUE: The face or dollar amount of a security.

PREFERRED STOCK: A class of stock with a claim on the company's earnings before dividends can be paid to common stockholders. Preferred stock usually has a priority over common stock if the company liquidates.

PREMIUM: The amount by which a security is selling above its par value. Can also refer to the premium bond issuers or stock buyers will pay to get their hands on the security.

PRE-RETIREMENT INCOME: The last salary you earn before you retire. Pension plans use this figure to determine benefits. You can judge the value of any retirement plan by how much of your pre-retirement salary it replaces.

PRICE-EARNINGS RATIO: You can find the price-earnings ratio by dividing the price of a share of stock by the earnings per share for a twelve-month period. For example: a stock selling for $50 a share and earning $2.50 a share has a price-earnings ratio of twenty to one.

PRIME RATE: The interest rate banks charge their best customers. Important as an indicator as to which way interest rates are headed.

PROFIT-SHARING PLAN: A retirement plan in which the company makes contributions depending on its profits. The employer has no obligation to make a contribution and, in most cases, it can't unless the company makes a profit in that year. Your benefit will be whatever the money in your account will buy when you retire.

PROSPECTUS: The booklet that offers new securities to the public. It tells you all about the company, what they intend to do with the money, and the important things you need to know before you invest. It is required under the Securities Act of 1933.

PURCHASING POWER: The value of a unit of money or other asset measured by the goods and services it can purchase. Your purchasing power increases when the same amount of money will buy more goods and services, and it falls when it takes more money to purchase the same amount of goods and services.

PUT: An option to sell a specified number of shares at a definite price within a specified period of time. The opposite of a call.

RATINGS: Usually refers to a bond's quality. The two nationally recognized ratings are from Moody's Investor Service and Standard and Poor's (S&P). The top three grades you should be looking for are AAA-prime grade, AA-excellent grade and A-high grade.

RECESSION: A period during which unemployment is usually on the rise, business slows, and our standard of living declines.

RED HERRING: Named because of the red ink on the cover, it is used as a preliminary prospectus to obtain an indication of interest from the public of a new issue.

REGISTERED REPRESENTATIVE: A full-time stockbroker who is licensed with an exchange to do business with the public. Also known as an account executive or customer's broker.

REPLACEMENT RATIO: The difference between your last working salary and your income in retirement. For example, suppose your last working salary was $25,000. If your retirement income is $6,250, your replacement ratio is 25%. Social Security now averages somewhere between 21-33%, depending on your last working salary. Usually the higher your pre-retirement salary, the lower your replacement ratio in retirement.

REVENUE BOND: A municipal security backed by and expected to repay the bondholder with earnings or revenues of a project, such as tolls from a bridge.

RISK: The possibility of a loss when you save or invest your money. Usually the greater the risk the higher the rewards.

ROLL OVER IRA: An IRA you establish to "roll over" the money from your employer's retirement plan. You can roll over any amount and continue to delay taxes, but you must roll over the money within 60 days of receipt to avoid paying income taxes in the year you receive the money.

ROUND LOT: The regular size stock transaction (100 or more shares) that does not incur special charges.

SALES CHARGE: The cost or sales commission you pay to buy or sell stocks, mutual funds, annuities, or other investments. The sales cost is taken off the top of your investment so that your actual investment is less than the money you invest.

SEC: The Securities and Exchange Commission, established by Congress in the 1930s to help protect investors. It is the watchdog over much of the securities business.

SECURED LOAN: Loan for which the collateral is a pledge to guarantee its repayment.

SELF-EMPLOYED INCOME: Income earned when you work for yourself or with a partner in business. You pay self-employment rates for your Social Security contribution, which are much higher than employees with the same income. Self-employed individuals can open a Keogh plan and an IRA.

SEP/IRA: Known as a Simplified Employee Pension, SEP/IRAs allow employer contributions of up to $25,000 or more into the employee's individual IRA. With an SEP/IRA you can also open your own regular IRA.

SHORT SALE: When you sell a stock you don't own in the belief that the price will go down and you can buy it back at a profit. When you buy a stock and invest in the stock market you are said to have gone "long." You are now buying before you sell, the opposite of a short position.

SPECULATION: Any investment made with the idea of making a profit from a change in price. Usually associated with a high-risk investment where large profits are expected in a short time.

SPREAD: The difference between what the seller wants and the buyer is willing to pay. Usually refers to unlisted stocks and bonds. The spread is the difference between the bid price and the ask price.

STOCK DIVIDEND: A dividend paid in securities rather than cash.

STOP-LOSS ORDER: Instructions given to a broker or bank to sell your investment if the price drops to a pre-set level. The stop-loss order then becomes a market order and your investment is sold as soon as a buyer can be found.

STREET NAME: If you buy securities from your broker they will normally be held in the name of the broker rather than in your name. They are said to be held in Street Name. If you want to hold your own securities, be sure to tell your broker.

SUMMARY PLAN DESCRIPTION: A booklet your employer is required by law to give you when you join your company retirement plan or whenever you ask for one. The booklet, which is to be written in "easy to understand" English, tells you how your retirement plan works, how you can benefit during your employment, and how to determine your benefits if you leave the company or retire.

SUPPLY OF MONEY: Amount of money in the banking system. The Fed is using the money supply as a way of determining future interest rates.

TAX CREDIT: The best way to save taxes! A tax credit is a dollar-for-dollar reduction in your tax bill. If you have a $100 tax credit you can take $100 off the amount of money you would otherwise send the IRS at tax time.

TAX DEFERRAL: The delaying of a tax liability. The IRA is a good example. You don't avoid taxes with an IRA; you delay them until you retire.

TAX EQUITY AND FISCAL RESPONSIBILITY ACT OF 1982: Called TEFRA, this law reduced our deductions for medical expenses and casualty losses and increased Keogh plan contri-

butions up to $30,000 a year. The law included a withhold-
ing tax on retirement plan benefits under pensions and
IRAs, but the withholding on dividends and interest was
voted down by Congress before it could take effect.

TAX-FREE INCOME: Usually income or interest you receive from a
municipal bond. To be tax-free of both federal and state
income taxes, you must invest in municipal bonds issued by
the state in which you live.

TAX SHELTER: An investment (usually a limited partnership) that
provides tax deductions and/or tax deferral. Usually sold to
people in the high-tax brackets who can afford to lose their
money if the investment goes sour.

TAX SHELTERED ANNUITY: Called a TSA, this retirement savings
plan works much like an IRA but it's available only
to employees of nonprofit organizations, such as school-
teachers.

TEN-YEAR RULE: A rule of Social Security whereby a divorced
spouse must have been married for at least ten years prior to
the divorce to collect benefits on the work record of the
ex-spouse. Benefits are paid then only if the spouse has not
remarried.

THRIFT PLANS: An employer savings plan whereby you make
voluntary contributions into the plan and your employer
matches your money on some formula. For example: for
every dollar you contribute into the plan your employer
would put in fifty cents. The interest income or profits inside
the thrift plan are tax-deferred until the money is taken out.

TIME DEPOSIT: A bank or thrift deposit where you agree to leave
the money on deposit for a fixed number of months or years.
If you withdraw the money prior to the agreed date you can
face a substantial early withdrawal penalty.

TREASURY SECURITIES: This is the way our government borrows
money to keep its financial house of cards from collapsing
into a sea of red ink. T-bills are sold at public auction on a
discounted basis (sold for less than the face value of the
security and then redeemed at face value). Three-month and
six-month T-bills are usually auctioned weekly on Mondays.
The minimum investment is $10,000, with multiples of
$5,000 above that. Treasury notes mature in ten years or less,
Treasury bonds mature ten years or more after issue.

TRUSTEE: The person who controls the trust, often with powers to buy and sell investments for the trust. When you open an IRA, the trustee only holds the investments and reports the increase and decrease in the account.

UNDERWRITER: A security firm that purchases an issue of new stocks or bonds from the issuer and then reoffers them for sale to the public. Banks, now barred by law, expect to underwrite municipal bonds as a first step back to becoming full underwriters of stocks and bonds.

UNEARNED INCOME: For tax purposes, this means interest, dividends, capital gains, rental income, and other forms of non-business income. You cannot make contributions to an IRA or Keogh plan with unearned income.

UNLISTED: A security not listed on a stock bond exchange.

VARIABLE ANNUITY: An annuity that's invested in a portfolio of stocks or other investments that can rise or fall with the market. Unlike a fixed annuity, there are no guarantees as to the value of principal since the portfolio performance will vary.

VESTING: Your right to receive your employer's contributions and the earned interest in the retirement plan when you change jobs prior to retirement. The vesting schedule is based on years of service. The law now requires that you be 100% vested after fifteen years' service. Until that time you earn "fractional vesting." You can find out, from your *Summary Plan Description* booklet, how much vesting you have earned and how much money you can take with you if you change jobs.

WARRANT: The right to purchase securities at a stipulated price within a specified time limit. Often warrants are offered with securities as an inducement to buy.

WITHDRAWAL PENALTIES: If you agree to lock up your money in a time deposit for a fixed number of months or years you can be charged a withdrawal penalty if you take out the money before the end of your time deposit.

WHOLE LIFE INSURANCE: See cash-value life insurance.

YIELD: The interest or dividend you expect to earn as a percentage of the current market value of your investment. After-tax yield is the return after income taxes, if any, have been subtracted.

ZERO COUPON BONDS: A bond that does not pay annual interest and is issued at a discount (very low dollar) price. The return on the bond is strictly the compounding effect of the stated interest rate over the life of the bond. Like U.S. Savings bonds, where for $18.75 you can buy a $25 bond, a zero coupon bond can cost $4,500 and in seventeen years hand you back $30,000.

APPENDICES

Where to Go for Help
Here are some books and folders that are worth writing for. Most of the material is free, but often limited to single copies only.

U.S. Government

Internal Revenue Service
111 Constitution Ave., N.W.
Office of Public Affairs
Washington, DC 20224
   Ask your local office or write Washington for publication #590, *Tax Information on Individual Retirement Arrangements* (IRAs). For Keogh plans, ask for publication #560, *Tax Information on Self-employed Retirement Plans.*

Office of Personal Management
(formerly Civil Service Commission)
Retirement Bureau
Washington, DC 20415
   If you work for the federal government this is the place to write about your retirement benefits. The Retirement Bureau will not give specific information by telephone. You must request information by writing.

Pension Benefit Guaranty Corporation
2020 K Street, N.W.
Washington, DC 20006

If your pension plan terminates or is about to terminate, contact the PBGC. This agency may continue to pay the benefits after your pension plan ends. Be sure to send in the full information about your company and your plan and ask for their booklets on guaranteeing pension benefits. Ask for their free book, *Your Guaranteed Pensions.*

Railroad Retirement Board
425 13th Street, N.W.
Washington, DC 20036

The Railroad Retirement Board, created one year before Social Security, provides basically the same retirement benefits but under a different bureaucracy. RRB has 80 district offices to provide information and process railroad retirement claims.

Small Business Administration
1441 L Street, N.W.
Washington, DC 20416

The Small Business Administration has ten regional offices in Boston, New York, Philadelphia, Atlanta, Chicago, Kansas City, Dallas, Denver, Seattle, and San Francisco. You can get information on SBA loans to help you start a business or find out about business reports by contacting any SBA office.

Social Security Administration
Department of Health, Education, and Welfare
Baltimore, MD 21235

The Social Security Administration provides services through district and branch offices and teleservice centers. If you are within five years of retirement, ask your local office to give you a status of your employment record. You can also ask for an "estimate of benefits" based on your past record. Ask for a copy of their booklets about Social Security. A good one for women is *A Woman's Guide to Social Security.*

Superintendent of Documents
U.S. Government Printing Office
Washington, DC 20402

The U.S. Department of Commerce publishes reports on a wide range of saving, investment, and money management topics. The reports are inexpensive, you can often find them at local libraries, or you can send in for a list of publications.

Federal Reserve Bank

For information about buying Treasury bills, notes, and bonds, either in person or by mail, write for *Buying Treasury Securities at Federal Reserve Banks,* Federal Reserve Bank, Public Relations Department, Box 27622, Richmond, VA 23261. For more information, write for *U.S. Treasury Securities,* Federal Reserve Bank, Securities Department, Station "K," Dallas, TX 75222.

U.S. Department of Labor
Pension and Welfare Benefit Programs
Office of Communications, Room N4662
200 Constitution Avenue, N.W.
Washington, DC 20216

For information regarding your private pension rights and an explanation of the federal laws about company retirement plans, this is the place to write.

Veterans Administration
Central Office
Washington, DC 20420

There are over fifty regional offices to provide information related to veterans. Because of the cutbacks contained in the federal budget, you should check as far in advance as you can to determine if you still qualify for benefits.

Other Helpful Information

American Bar Association
Circulation Department
1155 East 60th Street
Chicago, IL 60637

A new forty-one-page booklet explains your rights over age fifty. This is an excellent booklet on the legal steps you can take to protect yourself. You must send $2 to the ABA for each book you request.

Chicago Board of Options Exchange
LaSalle at Jackson
Chicago, IL 60604
A good place to find out about stock index options, how options are traded and what you need to know before you buy an option.

College for Financial Planning
9725 E Hampden Avenue
Denver, CO 80231
The college is an independent, nonprofit, educational institution that trains and tests candidates for the degree of Certified Financial Planner (CFP). You can write for a directory in your area and find out more about financial planners from the college. If you decide to use a financial planner, check to see if he or she is a Certified Financial Planner.

National Association of Securities Dealers (NASD)
1735 K Street, N.W.
Washington, DC 20006
The NASD is an association of brokers and dealers in the over-the-counter securities market. You can write for reports and information on unlisted securities, about the automated quote system (NASDAQ), and on how securities are bought and sold when they are not listed on a major exchange.

Runzheimer and Company
555 Skokie Blvd., Suite 245
Northbrook, IL 60062
A Pre-retirement Counseling Checklist, a valuable aid in making early retirement decisions, is available free from Runzheimer and Company.

Women's Pension Project
Pension Rights Center
Anne Moss, Project Director
1346 Connecticut Avenue, N.W.
Washington, DC 20036
Excellent source for information about retirement benefits for women. They offer a number of booklets and a newsletter. A good one is *A Guide to Understanding Your Pension Plan*. For a copy, send $2 to the center.

International Association for Financial Planning, Inc.
5775 Peachtree Dunwoody Road
Atlanta, GA 30342
The IAFP is a professional association for financial planners. It has a code of ethics and an examination to identify individuals who meet the highest standards in financial planning. You can send for a directory in your area or find out about financial planners from the association.

Investment Company Institute
1775 K Street, N.W.
Washington, DC 20006
This is the trade group for mutual funds. Write for a free directory of load and no-load mutual funds. This is the place to ask any questions you have of the mutual fund industry.

No-Load Mutual Fund Association
11 Pennsylvania Plaza, Suite 2204
New York, NY 10001
For a free directory of most no-load mutual funds with additional information on fund size, fees, redemption procedures, and service, write the association.

National Center for Financial Education
2107 Van Ness Avenue, Suite 308
San Francisco, CA 94109
This is a nonprofit organization where you can obtain information about financial planning. The center offers a monthly newsletter.

Publications to Help You with Financial Planning

Business Week magazine
1221 Avenue of the Americas
New York, NY 10020 $40 year
   Weekly business magazine about money, finances, and personal investing. Articles about industry, technology, and the economy.

Business Woman
5755 Cohasset Way
San Jose, CA 95153 $12 year
   A magazine for working women. Articles about saving, investing, and managing money.

Fact
711 Third Avenue
New York, NY 10017 $18 year
   The money management magazine. Information about how to manage your money, investment opportunities, what's new in business.

In Business
P.O. Box 323
Emmaus, PA 18049 $14 year
   Articles about business management, how to run a small business. Directed toward small businesses. Published every other month.

Inc.
38 Commercial Wharf
Boston, MA 02110 $18 year
   Directed toward well-established, existing businesses with more than $1 million in sales. The magazine is well written and a must if you are working for or own a small business.

The Jorgensen Report
80 S. Earley Street
Alexandria, VA 22308 $26 1 year, $45 2 years
   A nationwide monthly newsletter about saving money, taxes, and personal investing. The report comes in three parts: Current

Money Management; A Special Report (such as gold, IRAs, mutual funds, pensions); and A Special Feature (articles about current subjects (such as interest checking, SEP/IRAs, life insurance, discount brokers). For information or orders call toll free: 800-336-4776 (in Virginia call 703-823-6966).

Money magazine
Time, Inc.
3435 Wilshire Blvd.
Los Angeles, CA 90010 $24 year
 Articles about personal investing and money management. Covers mutual funds, stocks, bonds, IRAs, almost everything you need to know to stay on top of the money game.

Venture
35 W 45th Street
New York, NY 10036 $18 year
 The magazine for entrepreneurs. Articles about new business ventures, where you can start a business, and tips on where you can obtain government and private financing.

The Wall Street Journal
22 Cortland Street
New York, NY 10007 $47 6 months, $94 1 year, $172 2 years
 A daily newspaper about what's happening in business. You can buy the paper on a six-month or annual subscription basis. If you want to stay fully informed about all phases of the business world, *The Wall Street Journal* is a must.